NetLingo: The List
The Largest List of
Text & Chat Acronyms

by Erin Jansen

Disclaimer: This book is not recommended for
children under 14 due to mature and suggestive themes,
alcohol and drug references, intense use of profanity, and
a cornucopia of crude humor and sexual content.

The Largest List of Chat Acronyms & Text Shorthand

This guide is a print version of the NetLingo
List of Internet Acronyms and Text Shorthand.
To purchase additional copies of *NetLingo: The List*
and discover more, go to NetLingo.com :-)

The Largest List of Chat Acronyms & Text Shorthand

"Speak geek like a net native with NetLingo."
- *USA Today*

"The NetLingo guide to acronyms is super!"
- *People magazine*

"Start improving your cyber vocabulary with the NetLingo list of abbreviations." - *Real Simple*

"No acronym goes unexplained."
- *Computer Currents*

"NetLingo offers layman's terminology that will draw you in instead of driving you away." - *The Net*

"Fast relief from confusing Internet jargon."
- *The London Times*

"If you're baffled by Internet slang, NetLingo is a must."
- *BBC*

"As geek chic takes hold of the technology-obsessed culture, geek-speak seeps into everyday language."
- *The New York Times*

"NetLingo defines the new vocabulary surrounding the technology and community of the Web. Want to know the meaning of a word? This is the place to find out."
- *Fortune*

"One of the 100 best websites, NetLingo is a living dictionary devoted to the often cryptic and comedic vocabulary of the Internet, which is evolving at record speed." - *PC Magazine*

As featured on: Good Morning America, CNN, MSNBC, Fox News, NBC, CBS, Oxygen Network, Martha Stewart Show, Disney, NPR, *The Wall Street Journal* and more :-)

The Largest List of Chat Acronyms & Text Shorthand

Content matters

Hi!
Welcome to the weird, wonderful world of online jargon ;-)
Not only has the Internet and texting changed the way we
communicate, it has spawned an entirely new language
that is growing every day.

In an age where everything from job searching to dating
is interactive, knowing how to communicate in your online
life is a must. There are new technologies, new online
services, and new lingo created every day. If you think it's
tough to keep up with it all, you're not alone.

That's why there is NetLingo, to keep track of new terms
and organize it in a way that is useful to you. Whether
you're a professional who feels like you're on information
overload, or a power user who wants more, or a parent
who wants to keep up with your kids, NetLingo can help.

NetLingo.com is the leading Internet Dictionary that
explains the online world of business, technology and
communication. We offer products and services to help
you stay up-to-date in your online world. Written by me,
a woman using layman's language, my purpose is to
educate, entertain, and empower you!

This revised edition of *NetLingo: The List* defines the
crazy array of letters, numbers and symbols that
comprise our new conversations. Known as acronyms,
abbreviations, SMS talk and leetspeak, these terms are
used by millions of people in a variety of online settings.
Enjoy!
Erin Jansen
Editor and Publisher

What are acronyms and why are they so popular?

With millions of people texting and instant messaging every day, it's no wonder you've seen this cryptic looking code. Acronyms are an integral part of computer culture and grew rapidly on the Internet. Now, along with an alphabet soup of abbreviations and symbolic messages, this online jargon has become a language of its own.

So what are acronyms? Shorthand? Leetspeak? How do you begin to understand a new language?

Let's start with the basics: An acronym is derived from the first letters of a phrase and is pronounced as a new word, for example POTATO stands for "People Over Thirty Acting Twenty One" and is pronounced "potato."

Shorthand refers to an abbreviation, or initialism, that is pronounced by saying the letters one-by-one, for example FYI is pronounced "F-Y-I" and BRB is pronounced "B-R-B". There are, of course, exceptions. Some acronyms go both ways, such as FAQ, which can be pronounced "fak" or "F-A-Q".

It should also be noted that acronyms are generally typed IN ALL CAPS (not to be confused with SHOUTING) whereas shorthand is often typed in all lowercase.

Now let's start to mix things up. Sometimes the shorthand isn't shorter than the original phrase, for example "dewd" means "dude" and "kewl" means "cool" and :::poof::: means "I'm gone".

Leetspeak is a type of symbolic jargon in which you replace regular letters with other keyboard characters to form words, for example:

- backward and forward slashes create this shape "/\\/\\" to stand for the letter M;
- numbers and symbols often replace the letters they resemble (for example the term "leetspeak" is written as "!337$p34k");
- letters can be substituted for other letters that might sound alike (such as "ph" is transposed with "f" so "phear" is used instead of "fear"); and
- common typing errors such as "teh" instead of "the" and "pwn" instead of "own" are left uncorrected.

The result is a dynamic written language that eludes conformity or consistency. In fact, the culture of online jargon encourages new forms of expression and users will often award each other's individual creativity.

So what makes texting and instant messaging so popular? In short, it's fast, cheap, and cool.

Texting lets you finalize last-minute plans, track down friends, send pictures, correspond while traveling, and pass on information with just a few clicks of the cell phone keypad. IM lets you have real-time conversations with friends or colleagues or several people at once on your computer screen. Texing and IM are popular because they are private: no one can hear you "talking." Acronyms and smileys are popular because they're short and they bring emotional expression into a written world.

Face it, communication is changing. It's becoming quicker and less formal, and while it's impossible to capture every instance of every text message out there, this is the definitive list. Many people at some point will use or see a variation of a term in this book, often without the vowels so as to keep the text or IM short. Such as: omw, meet me n frnt pls -or- got ur vm, thx 4 info, ttyl

Think it's tough to understand? It's not, take this test:

Cna yuo raed tihs? Olny 55 plepoe out of 100 can. i cdnuolt blveiee taht I cluod aulaclty uesdnatnrd waht I was rdanieg. The phaonmneal pweor of the hmuan mnid, aoccdrnig to a rscheearch at Cmabrigde Uinervtisy, it dseno't mtaetr in waht oerdr the ltteres in a wrod are, the olny iproamtnt tihng is taht the frsit and lsat ltteer be in the rghi t pclae. The rset can be a taotl mses and you can sitll raed it whotuit a pboerlm. Tihs is bcuseae the huamn mnid deos not raed ervey lteter by istlef, but the wrod as a wlohe. Azanmig huh?

Like most new things, communicating in abbreviations may seem strange at first but then fun after awhile. *NetLingo: The List* will help you translate the chat acronyms and text shorthand you come across while traversing the online world.

Each term seen here in *NetLingo: The List* is further defined on NetLingo.com. I encourage you to go to the website to learn more and see examples of how this language is used and submit your own terms. Here is a direct link to the NetLingo List of Chat Acronyms and Text Shorthand: http://www.netlingo.com/acronyms.php

SYMBOLS & NUMBERS

!	I have a comment
^5	High Five
^RUP^	Read Up Please
^URS	Up Yours
*$	Starbucks
**//	it means wink wink, nudge nudge
,!!!!	Talk to the hand
02 or m.02	Your (or my) two cents worth
10Q	Thank you
1174	Nude club
121	One to one
1337	Elite -or- leet -or- L337
14	it refers to the fourteen words
143	I love you
1432	I Love You Too
14AA41	One for All and All for One
182	I hate you
187	it means murder/ homicide
190	hand
1daful	it means wonderful
2	it means to, too, two
20	Location
24/7	Twenty Four Seven, all the time
2b	To be
2B or not 2B	To Be Or Not To Be
2b@	To Be At
2BZ4UQT	Too Busy For You Cutey
2B~not2B	To be or not to be

2d4	To die for
2day	Today
2DLoo	Toodle oo
2G2B4G	Too Good To Be Forgotten
2G2BT	Too Good To Be True
2moro	Tomorrow
2nite	Tonight
2QT	Too Cute
2U2	To You Too
303	Mom
4	For, Four
404	I haven't a clue
411	Information
420	Marijuana
459	I love you
4COL	For Crying Out Loud
4EAE	ForEver And Ever
4eva, 4ever	Forever
4NR	Foreigner
4Q	F*** You
511	Too much information
53X	Sex
5FS	5 Finger Salute
747	Let's Fly
8	it means oral sex, the new 69
831	I Love You
86	Out of, over, get rid of, or kicked out
88	Hugs and kisses
8t	it means it
9	Parent is watching
99	Parent is no longer watching

The Largest List of Chat Acronyms & Text Shorthand

::poof::	I'm gone
<3	it's a heart
?	I have a question
?^	Wanna hook up?
@	it means at
@+	French equivalent of CUL8R
@TEOTD	At The End Of The Day

_____
_____
_____
_____
_____
_____
_____
_____
_____
_____
_____
_____
_____
_____
_____
_____
_____
_____
_____
_____
_____

-A-

A/N	Author's Note
A/S/L/P	Age/Sex/Location/Picture
A2D	Agree to Disagree
A3	Anytime, Anyplace, Anywhere
AAAAA	American Association Against Acronym Abuse
AAF	As A Friend -or- Always And Forever
AAK	Asleep At Keyboard
AAMOF	As A Matter Of Fact
AAMOI	As A Matter Of Interest
AAR	At Any Rate
AAR8	At Any Rate
AAS	Alive And Smiling
AATK	Always At The Keyboard
AAYF	As Always, Your Friend
AB	Ass Backwards -or- Ah Bless
ab/abt	about
ABC	Always Be Creating / Collaborating / Communicating
ABITHIWTITB	A Bird In The Hand Is Worth Two In The Bush
ABK	Always Be Knolling
ABT2	About To
ACD	Alt Control Delete
ACE	Access Control Entry
ACK	Acknowledgement
ACORN	A Completely Obsessive Really Nutty person

ADAD	Another Day Another Dollar
ADBB	All Done Bye Bye
add	Address
addy	address
ADIDAS	All Day I Dream About Sex
ADIH	Another Day In Hell
ADIP	Another Day In Paradise
ADM	Aye Dios Mio
AND	Any Day Now
ADR	Address
ADVD	Advised
AEAP	As Early As Possible
AFAGAY	A Friend As Good As You
AFAHMASP	A Fool And His Money Are Soon Parted
AFAIC	As Far As I'm Concerned
AFAICS	As Far As I Can See
AFAICT	As Far As I Can Tell
AFAIK	As Far As I Know
AFAIR	As Far As I Remember
AFAIU	As Far As I Understand
AFAIUI	As Far As I Understand It
AFAP	As Far As Possible
AFAYC	As Far As You're Concerned
AFC	Away From Computer
AFDN	Any F***ing Day Now
AFGO	Another F***ing Growth Opportunity
AFIAA	As Far As I Am Aware
AFINIAFI	A Friend In Need Is A Friend Indeed
AFJ	April Fools Joke
AFK	Away From Keyboard -or- A Free Kill

AFPOE	A Fresh Pair Of Eyes
AFT	About F***ing Time
AFU	All F***ed Up
AFW	Away From Window
AFZ	Acronym Free Zone
AGB	Almost Good Bridge
AGKWE	And God Knows What Else
AI	Artificial Intelligence -or- As If
AIAMU	And I'm A Monkey's Uncle
aight	all right
AIH	As It Happens
AIMB	As I Mentioned Before
AIMP	Always In My Prayers
AISB	As I Said Before
AISE	As I Said Earlier
AISI	As I See It
AITR	Adult In The Room
AKA or a.k.a.	Also Known As
ALAP	As Late As Possible
alcon	All Concerned
ALOL	Actually Laughing Out Loud
ALOTBSOL	Always Look On The Bright Side Of Life
ALTG	Act Locally, Think Globally
ALW	Ain't Life Wonderful
AMA	Ask Me Anything
AMAP	As Many (or Much) As Possible
AMBW	All My Best Wishes
AMF	Adios Mother F***er
AML	All My Love
AMRMTYFTS	All My Roommates Thank You For The Show

ANFAWFOS	And Now For A Word From Our Sponsor
ANFSCD	And Now For Something Completely Different
ANGB	Almost Nearly Good Bridge
AOAS	All Of A Sudden
AOB	Abuse Of Bandwidth
AON	Apropos Of Nothing
AOR	Agency Of Record
AOYP	Angel On Your Pillow
AP	Apple Pie
AR	Action Required
AS	Ape Sh** -or- Another Subject
ASAFP	As Soon As F***ing Possible
ASAMOF	As A Matter Of Fact
ASAP	As Soon As Possible
ASAYGT	As Soon As You Get This
ASL	Age/Sex/Location
ASLMH	Age/Sex/Location/Music/Hobbies
ATAB	Ain't That A Bitch
ATC	Any Two Cards
ATM	At The Moment, Automated Teller Machine
ATSL	Along The Same Line
ATST	At The Same Time
ATW	All The Web, Around The Web, All The Way, At The Weekend
ATWD	Agree That We Disagree
AUNT	And U Know This
AUNTM	And U Know This Man
AWC	After While, Crocodile

AWGTHTGTTA	Are We Going To Have To Go Through This Again
AWHFY	Are We Having Fun Yet?
AWLTP	Avoiding Work Like The Plague
AWNIAC	All We Need Is Another Chair
AWOL	Absent Without Leave
AWTTW	A Word To The Wise
ax	it means across
AYC	Aren't You Clever / Cheeky
AYCE	All You Can Eat
AYFKMWTS	Are You F***ing Kidding Me With This Sh**
AYK	As You Know
AYMM	Are You My Mother
AYOR	At Your Own Risk
AYSOS	Are You Stupid Or Something
AYTMTB	And You're Telling Me This Because
AYV	Are You Vertical?

_____

_____

_____

_____

_____

_____

_____

_____

_____

_____

_____

_____

-B-

B	Be
B&E	Breaking & Entering
B&F	Back and Forth
B/C	Because
B/W	Between
B2A	Business-to-Anyone
B2B	Business-to-Business
B2B2C	Business-to-Business-to-Consumer
B2C	Business-to-Consumer
B2D	Business-to-Distributor
B2E	Business-to-Employee
B2G	Business-to-Government
B4	Before
B4N	Bye For Now
B4U	Before You
B4YKI	Before You Know It
B@U, BAK@U	Back at You
BABY	Being Annoyed By You
BAC	Bad Ass Chick
BAG	Busting A Gut -or- Big Ass Grin
BAK	Back At Keyboard
BAMF	Bad Ass Mother F***er
banana	it means penis
BARB	Buy Abroad but Rent in Britain
BAU	Business As Usual
BB	Be Back -or- Buzzard Breath -or- Blessed Be
BB4N	Bye Bye for Now

BBAMFIC	Big Bad Ass Mother F***er In Charge
BBB	Bye Bye Babe -or- Boring Beyond Belief
BBBG	Bye Bye Be Good
BBFBBM	Body By Fisher, Brains By Mattel
BBFN	Bye Bye for Now
BBIAB	Be Back In A Bit
BBIAF	Be Back In A Few
BBIAS	Be Back In A Sec
BBIAW	Be Back In A While
BBL	Be Back Later
BBMFIC	Big Bad Mother F***er In Charge
BBQ	Barbeque
BBR	Burnt Beyond Repair
BBS	Be Back Soon -or Bulletin Board Service
BBSD	Be Back Soon Darling
BBSL	Be Back Sooner or Later
BBT	Be Back Tomorrow
BBW	Big Beautiful Woman -or- Big Black Woman
BC	Because
BCBG	Bon Chic Bon Genre -or- Belle Cul Belle Geulle
BCBS	Big Company, Big School
BCNU	Be Seeing You
bcoz	because
BD	Big Deal -or- Baby Dance -or- Brain Drain
BDBI5M	Busy Daydreaming Back In 5 Minutes
BDC	Big Dumb Company -or- Big Dot Com
BDN	Big Damn Number
BDOA	Brain Dead On Arrival
BDSM	Bondage, Dominance, Sadism, Masochism
BEG	Big Evil Grin

beos	Nudge
BF	Boyfriend -or- Best Friend
BFD	Big F***ing Deal -or- Big F***ing Disaster
BFE	Bum F*** Egypt
BFF	Best Friends Forever
BFFN	Best Friends For Now
BFFTTE	Best Friends Forever Til The End
BFG	Big F***ing Gun
BFN	Bye For Now
BFR	Big F***ing Rock
BG	Be Good
BGF	Best GirlFriend
BHAG	Big Hairy Audacious Goal
BHG	Big Hearted Guy / Girl
BHIMBGO	Bloody Hell, I Must Be Getting Old
BHOF	Bald Headed Old Fart
BI	Business Intelligence
BI5	Back In Five
BIBI	Bye Bye
BIBO	Beer In, Beer Out
BIF	Basis In Fact -or- Before I Forget
BIL	Brother-In-Law -or- Boss Is Listening
BIO	Bring It On
BIOIYA	Break It Off In Your Ass
BION	Believe It Or Not
BIOYA	Blow It Out Your Ass
BIOYE	Blow It Out Your Ear
BIOYIOP	Blow It Out Your I/O Port
BIOYN	Blow it Out Your Nose
BITCH	Basically In The Clear Homey
BITD	Back In The Day

BITFOB	Bring It The F*** On, Bitch
BJ	Blow Job
BKA	Better Known As
BL	Belly Laughing
BLBBLB	Back Like Bull, Brain Like Bird
Blkbry	Blackberry
BLZRD	it means blizzard
BM	Byte Me
BMF	Bad Mother F***er
BMGWL	Busting My Gut With Laughter
BMOC	Big Man On Campus
BMOF	Bite Me Old Fart
BMOTA	Byte Me On The Ass
BMS	Baby Making Sex
BMW	B*tch, Moan, Whine
BN	Been -or- Being
BNDN	Been Nowhere Done Nothing
BNF	Big Name Fan
BO	Bug Off -or- Body Odor
BOAISY	Bend Over And I'll Show You
BOB	Battery Operated Boyfriend
BOBFOC	Body Off Baywatch, Face Off Crimewatch
BOCTAAE	But Of Course There Are Always Exceptions
BOD	Benefit of the Doubt -or- Board Of Directors
BOFH	Bastard Operator From Hell
BOHICA	Bend Over Here It Comes Again
BON	Believe it Or Not
book	it means cool
BOTEC	Back Of The Envelope Calculation

BOTL	Bra On The Loose
BOTOH	But On The Other Hand
BPLM	Big Person Little Mind
BR	Bathroom
BRB	Be Right Back
BRIC	Brazil, Russia, India, China
BRL	Belly Roll Laughs
BRO	Be Right Over
BRT	Be Right There
BRUF	Big Requirements Up Front
BS	Big Smile -or- Bull Sh** -or- Brain Strain
BSAAW	Big Smile And A Wink
BSBD&NE	Book Smart, Brain Dead & No Experience
BSEG	Big Sh** Eating Grin
BSF	But Seriously, Folks
BSOD	Blue Screen of Death
BT	Byte This
BTA	But Then Again -or- Before The Attacks
BTD	Bored To Death
BTDT	Been There Done That
BTDTGTS	Been There, Done That, Got The T-shirt
BTFLDY	it means beautiful day
BTFO	Back The F*** Off -or- Bend The F*** Over
BTHOOM	Beats The Heck Out Of Me
BTN	Better Than Nothing
BTOIYA	Be There Or It's Your Ass
BTR	Better
BTSOOM	Beats The Sh** Out Of Me
BTTT	Back To The Top -or- Bump To The Top
BTW	By The Way -or- Bring The Wheelchair
BTWBO	Be There With Bells On

BTWITIAILWU	By The Way I Think I Am In Love With You
BTYC	Better Than You Can
BTYD	Better Than You Do
BUFF	Big Ugly Fat F***
buhbye	bye bye
bump	Bring Up My Post
BW	Best Wishes
BWDIK	But What Do I Know
BWI	But What If
BWL	Bursting With Laughter
BWO	Black, White or Other
BWTM	But Wait, There's More
BYAM	Between You And Me
BYKI	Before You Know It
BYKT	But You Knew That
BYOA	Bring Your Own Advil
BYOB	Bring Your Own Bottle / Beer
BYOD	Bring Your Own Device
BYOW	Build Your Own Website -or- Bring Your Own Wine
BYTME	Better You Than ME
BZ	Busy

_____
_____
_____
_____
_____
_____
_____

-C-

C	it means see
c ya	see ya
c%d	it means could
c%l	it means cool
C&G	Chuckle and Grin
C-P	Sleepy
C-T	City
C/P	Cross Post
C/S	Change of Subject
C4N	Ciao For Now
CAAC	Cool As A Cucumber
CAS	Crack A Smile
CB	Chat Brat -or- Coffee Break -or Call Back
CBB	Can't Be Bothered
CBF	Can't Be F***ed
CBJ	Covered Blow Job
CBM	Covered By Medicare
cc	carbon copy
CD9	Code 9 - it means parents are around
CF	Coffee Freak -or- Cluster F***
CFV	Call For Vote
CHA	Click Here Asshole
chln	it means chilling
CIAO	Goodbye (in Italian)
CICO	Coffee In, Coffee Out
CICYHW	Can I Copy Your Home Work
CID	Consider It Done -or- Crying In Disgrace
CIL	Check In Later

CINBA	Clad In Naught But Air
CIO	Check It Out -or- Chief Information Officer -or- Chief Internet Officer
CLD	it means cold
CLM	Career Limiting Move
CM	Call Me
CMAO	Chortling My Ass Off
CMAP	Cover My Ass Partner
CMB	Call Me Back
CMF	Count My Fingers
CMIW	Correct Me if I'm Wrong
CMU	Crack Me Up
CN	Can
CNP	Continued in Next Post
COB	Close Of Business
COBRAS	Come On By Right After School
COD	Change Of Dressing
Cof$	Church of Scientology
COL	Chuckling / Chortling Out Loud
coo	short for cool
COS	Change Of Subject -or- because
COT	Circle Of Trust
CPG	Consumer Packaged Goods
CQRT	Security
CRAFT	Can't Remember A F***ing Thing
CRAP	Cheap Redundant Assorted Products
CRAT	Can't Remember A Thing
CRAWS	Can't Remember Anything Worth A Sh**
CRB	Come Right Back
CRBT	Crying Real Big Tears
CRD	Caucasian Rhythm Disorder / Deficiency

CRDTCHCK	Credit Check
CRS	Can't Remember Sh**
CRTLA	Can't Remember the Three-Letter Acronym
CS	Career Suicide
CS&F	Cute Sexy & Funny
CSA	Cool Sweet Awesome
CSABR	Continued Success And Best Regards
CSL	Can't Stop Laughing
CSN	Chuckle, Snicker, Grin
CT	Can't Talk -or- Can't Text
CTA	Call To Action
CTC	Care To Chat -or- Contact -or- Choking The Chicken
CTFD	Calm The F*** Down
CTFO	Come The F*** On
CTFU	Cracking The F*** Up
CTMQ	Chuckle To Myself Quietly
CTO	Check This Out
CU	See You -or- Cracking Up
CU46	See You For Sex
CUATSC	See You At The Senior Center
CUATU	See You Around The Universe
CUL	See You Later
CUL8R	See You Later
CULA	See You Later Alligator
CUNS	See You In School
CUNT	See You Next Time / Tuesday -or- Can't Understand Newest Text
CUOL	See You OnLine
CUPL	Couple
CUWTA	Catch Up With The Acronyms

CUZ	Because
CWOT	Complete Waste Of Time
CWYL	Chat With You Later
CX	Cancelled
CY	Calm Yourself
CYA	Cover Your Ass -or- See Ya
CYE	Check your Email
CYL	See You Later
CYM	Check Your Mail
CYO	See You Online
CYOH	Create Your Own Happening
CYT	See You Tomorrow

-D-

D	Dad -or- it means the
D&M	Deep & Meaningful
d/c	disconnected
d00d	dude, also seen as dood
D2D	Developer-to-Developer
D8	Date
da	there
DAMHIKT	Don't Ask Me How I Know That
DARFC	Ducking And Running For Cover
DBA	Doing Business As
DBABAI	Don't Be A Bitch About It
DBBSWF	Dream Boat Body, Shipwreck Face
DBD	Don't Be Dumb
DBEYR	Don't Believe Everything You Read
DBMIB	Don't Bother Me I'm Busy
DD	Due Diligence
DDAS	Don't Do Anything Stupid
DDG	Drop Dead Gorgeous
DDSOS	Different Day, Same Old Sh**
DDWI	Don't Dick With It
def	Definitely
DEGT	Don't Even Go There
dem	them
DENIAL	Don't Even Notice I Am Lying
dese	these
DETI	Don't Even Think It
dewd	dude
dey	they

DF	Dear Friend
DFIK	Darn If I Know
DFLA	Disenhanced Four-Letter Acronym
DFTBA	Don't Forget To Be Awesome
DFU	Don't F*** Up
DFWLY	Don't Forget Who Loves You
DGA	Don't Go Anywhere
DGAF	Don't Give A F***
DGARA	Don't Give A Rat's Ass
DGT	Don't Go There
DGTG	Don't Go There Girlfriend
DGYF	Damn Girl You're Fine
DH	Dear Husband
DHYB	Don't Hold Your Breath
DIAF	Die In A Fire
DIC	Drunk In Charge
DIFBET	it means what's the difference between
DIKU	Do I Know You?
DILLIGAD	Do I Look Like I Give A Damn
DILLIGAS	Do I Look Like I Give A Sh**
DINK	Double Incomes, No Kids
DINR	Dinner
DIRFT	Do It Right the First Time
DISTO	Did I Say That Outloud?
DITR	Dancing In The Rain
ditto	same here
DITYID	Did I Tell You I'm Distressed
DIY	Do It Yourself
DJM	Don't Judge Me
DK	Don't Know
DKDC	Don't Know Don't Care

DL	Down Low -or- Download -or- Dead Link
DLTBBB	Don't Let The Bed Bugs Bite
DLTM	Don't Lie To Me
DM	Direct Message
DMI	Don't Mention It
DNBL8	Do Not Be Late
DNC	Does Not Compute
DND	Do Not Disturb
DNPMPL	Damn Near Pissed My Pants Laughing
DOA	Dead On Arrival
DOC	Drug Of Choice
DOE	Depends On Experience
DOEI	Goodbye (in Dutch)
doin	it means doing
DORD	Department Of Redundancy Department
DP	Domestic Partner
dps	Damage Per Second
DPUP	Don't Poop Your Pants
DQMOT	Don't Quote Me On This
DQYDJ	Don't Quit Your Day Job
DRB	Dirty Rat Bastard
DRCOWOTO	Don't Really Care One Way Or The Other
DRIB	Don't Read If Busy
DSTR8	Damn Straight
DTC	Deep Throaty Chuckle
DTF	Down To F***
DTK	Down To Kill
DTRT	Do The Right Thing
DUI	Driving Under the Influence
DUM	Do You Masturbate?
DUNA	Don't Use No Acronyms

dunno	don't know
DUR	Do You Remember
DURS	Damn You Are Sexy
DUSL	Do You Scream Loud?
DUST	Did You See That?
DW	Don't Worry
DW2H	Don't Work Too Hard
DWB	Don't Write Back
DWBH	Don't Worry Be Happy
DWH	During Work Hours
DWI	Driving While Intoxicated
DWPKOTL	Deep Wet Passionate Kiss On The Lips
DWS	Driving While Stupid
DWWWI	Surfing the World Wide Web while intoxicated
DWYM	Does What You Mean
DYAC	Damn You Auto Correct
DYFM	Dude You Fascinate Me
DYHAB	Do You Have A Boyfriend?
DYHAG	Do You Have A Girlfriend
DYJHIW	Don't You Just Hate It When...
DYLI	Do You Love It?
DYOFDW	Do Your Own F***ing Dirty Work
DYSTSOTT	Did You See The Size Of That Thing

_____
_____
_____
_____
_____
_____
_____

-E-

E123	Easy as One, Two, Three
E2HO	Each to His/Her Own
EABOS	Eat A Bag Of Sh**
EADD	Entrepreneurial Attention Deficit Disorder
EAK	Eating at Keyboard
EAPFS	Everything About Pittsburgh F***ing Sucks
ED	Erectile Dysfunction
EE	Electronic Emission
EE or EEs	Employee -or- Employees
effin	F***ing
EFT	Electronic Funds Transfer
EG	Evil Grin
EIP	Eggo Is Preggo
EL	Evil Laugh
ELOL	Evil Laugh Out Loud
EM	Excuse Me
EMA	E-Mail Address
EMBM	Early Morning Business Meeting
EMFBI	Excuse Me For Butting In
EMFJI	Excuse Me For Jumping In
EMI	Excuse My Ignorance
EML	Email Me Later
EMP	Eat My Pussy
EMRTW	Evil Monkey's Rule The World
EMSG	E-Mail Message
EOD	End Of Day -or- End Of Discussion
EOL	End Of Life
EOM	End Of Message

EOT	End Of Thread/Text/Transmission
ESAD	Eat Sh** And Die
ESADYFA	Eat Sh** And Die You F***ing Asshole
ESEMED	Every Second Every Minute Every Day
ESFOAD	Eat Sh** F***Off And Die
ESG	Environmental, Social, Governance
ESH	Experience, Strength, and Hope
ESMF	Eat Sh** Mother F***er
ESO	Equipment Smarter than Operator
ETA	Estimated Time of Arrival -or-
	Edited To Add
ETLAETLA	Extended Three-Letter Acronym
ETX	End of TeXt
every1	everyone
EVRE1	Every One
EWI	E-mailing While Intoxicated
EZ	Easy

_____
_____
_____
_____
_____
_____
_____
_____
_____
_____
_____
_____
_____

-F-

F	Friend
F2F	Face-to-Face, a.k.a. face time
F2Fmail	Face-to-Face mail
F2T	Free To Talk
FAB	Features Attributes Benefits
FAF	Find A Friend
FAH	F***ing A Hot
FAP	F***ing A Pissed
FAQL	Frequently Asked Questions List
FASB	Fast Ass Son Bitchii
FATM	Foaming At The Mouth
FAV	Favorite
FAWC	For Anyone Who Cares
FAWOMFT	Frequently Argued Waste Of My F***ing Time
FAY	F*** All Y'all
FB	F*** Buddy -or- FaceBook
FBI	F***ing Brilliant Idea -or- Female Body Inspector
FBKS	Failure Between Keyboard and Seat
FBOCD	Facebook Obsessive Compulsive Disorder
FCFS	First Come, First Served
FCOL	For Crying Out Loud
FCS	First Customer Ship
FDFF	Falling Down F***ing Funny
FDGB	Fall Down Go Boom
FE	Fatal Error

FEAR	Forget Everything And Run -or- Face Everything And Recover
FF	Friends Forever
FF&PN	Fresh Fields and Pastures New
FFA	Free For All
FFS	For F*** Sake
FFT	Food For Thought
FGDAI	Fuhgedaboudit -or- Forget About It
FIF	F*** I'm Funny
FIFO	First In, First Out
FIGJAM	F*** I'm Good Just Ask Me
FIGMO	F*** It Got My Orders
FIGS	French, Italian, German, Spanish
FIIK	F*** If I Know
FIL	Father-In-Law
FILF	Father I'd Like to F***
FILTH	Failed In London, Try Hong Kong
FINE	F***ed up, Insecure, Neurotic, Emotional -or- F*** It Never Ends
FISH	First in, Still Here
FITB	Fill In The Blanks
FKM	F*** 'Em
FLA	Four Letter Acronym
FLOTUS	First Lady Of The United States
FLUID	F***ing Look it Up, I Did
FML	F*** My Life
FMLTWIA	F*** Me Like The Whore I Am
FMTYEWTK	Far More Than You Ever Wanted To Know
FMUTA	F*** Me Up The Ass
FNG	F***ing New Guy

FO	F*** Off
FOAD	F*** Off And Die
FOAF	Friend Of A Friend
FOAG	F*** Off And Google
fob	the name for a tool or form of ID
FOC	Free of Charge
FOFL	Falling on Floor Laughing
FOGC	Fear Of Getting Caught
FOL	Fond of Leather
FOMC	Fell Off My Chair
FOMCL	Falling Off My Chair Laughing
FOMO	Fear Of Missing Out
FOMOF	Fear Of Missing Out on Football
FOOT	F*** Off Over There -or- go away
FORD	Found On Road Dead, Fixed Or Repaired Daily, F***ed Over Rebuilt Dodge
FOS	Full Of Sh**
FOUO	For Official Use Only
FPO	For Placement Only
FRED	F***ing Ridiculous Electronic Device
FRZN	it means freezing
FS	For Sale
FSBO	For Sale By Owner
FSR	For Some Reason
FSU	F*** Sh** Up
FTASB	Faster Than A Speeding Bullet
FTBL	Football
FTBOMH	From The Bottom Of My Heart
FTC	Failure To Communicate
FTE	Full Time Employee
FTF	F*** That's Funny -or- Face To Face

FTFO	IFor The Fun Of It -or- For The F*** Of It
FTL	Faster Than Light
FTLOG	For The Love Of God
FTN	F*** That Noise
FTR	For The Record
FTRF	F*** That's Really Funny
FTTB	For The Time Being
FTW	For The Win -or- F*** The World
FU2	F*** You Too
FUB	Fat Ugly Bastard
FUBAR	F***ed Up Beyond All Recognition / Repair
FUBB	F***ed Up Beyond Belief
FUBYOYO	F*** You Buddy You're On Your Own
FUD	Fear, Uncertainty, and Disinformation
FUJIMO	F*** You Jack I'm Movin' On
FUM	F***ed Up Mess
FUMF	Fat Ugly Mother F***er
FUPA	Fat Upper Pussy Area
FURTB	Filled Up and Ready To Burst
FUW	F*** You World -or- F*** You Weirdo
FWB	Friends With Benefits
FWD	Forward
FWIW	For What It's Worth -or- Forgot Where I Was
FWOT	F***ing Waste Of Time
FYA	For Your Amusement
FYC	For Your Consideration
FYE	For Your Edification
FYEO	For Your Eyes Only
FYF	From Your Friend
FYI	For Your Information
FYIFV	F*** You I'm Fully Vested

FYLTGE	From Your Lips To Gods Ears
FYM	For Your Misinformation
FYSBIGTBABN	Fasten Your Seat Belts It's Going To Be A Bumpy Night

_____

_____

_____

_____

_____

_____

_____

_____

_____

_____

_____

_____

_____

_____

_____

_____

_____

_____

_____

_____

-G-

G	Guess -or- Grin -or- Giggle
G1	Good One
G2G	Got to Go
G2GLYS	Got To Go Love Ya So
G4I	Go For It
G4N	Good For Nothing
G9	Genius
g98t	good night
GA	Go Ahead -or- Good Afternoon
GAB	Getting A Beer
GAFL	Get A F***ing Life
GAFYK	Get Away From Your Keyboard
GAGFI	Gives A Gay First Impression
GAHOY	Get A Hold Of Yourself
GAL	Get A Life
GALGAL	Give A Little Get A Little
GALHER	Get A Load of Her
GALHIM	Get A Load of Him
GANB	Getting Another Beer
GAP	Got A Pic -or- Gay Ass People
GAS	Got A Second?
gawd	God
GB	Good Bridge
GBG	Great Big Grin
GBH	Great Big Hug
GBTW	Get Back To Work
GC	Good Crib
GD&R	Grinning, Ducking and Running
GD&RF	Grinning, Ducking and Running Fast

GDI	God Damn It -or- God Damn Independent
GDW	Grin, Duck and Wave
GF	Girlfriend
GFF	Go F***ing Figure
GFI	Go For It
GFN	Gone For Now
GFON	Good For One Night
GFR	Grim File Reaper
GFTD	Gone For The Day
GFY	Good For You -or- Go F*** Yourself -or- Go Find Yourself
GFYMF	Go F*** Yourself Mother F***er
GG	Good Game -or- Gotta Go -or- Giggling
GGA	Good Game All
GGGG	God, God, God, God
GGN	Gotta Go Now
GGOH	Gotta Get Out of Here
GGP	Gotta Go Pee
GGPBL	Gotta Go, Pacemaker Battery Low
GGY	Go Google Yourself
GHM	God Help Me
GI	Google It
GIC	Gift In Crib
GIDK	Gee I Don't Know
GIGATT	God Is Good All The Time
GIGO	Garbage In, Garbage Out
GILF	Grandmother I'd Like to F***
GIST	Great Ideas for Starting Things
GIWIST	Gee, I Wish I'd Said That
GJ	Good Job

GJP	Good Job Partner
GL	Good Luck -or- Get Lost
GLA	Good Luck All
GLB	Good Looking Boy
GLBT	Gay, Lesbian, Bisexual, Transgender
GLG	Good Looking Girl
GLGH	Good Luck and Good Hunting
GLYASDI	God Loves You And So Do I
GM	Good Morning -or- Good Move
GMAB	Give Me A Break
GMAFB	Give Me A F***ing Break
GMILY	Good Morning I Love You
GMTA	Great Minds Think Alike
GMTA ASDO	Great Minds Think Alike, And So Do Ours
GMTFT	Great Minds Think For Themselves
GN	Good Night
gn8	good night
GNBLFY	Got Nothing But Love For You
GNOC	Get Naked On Cam
GNS	GangNam Style
GNSD	Good Night Sweet Dreams
GOB	Game On Bitches
GOI	Get Over It
GOK	God Only Knows
GOL	Giggling Out Loud
GOLF	Grateful Of Lovely Family / Friends
GOOD job	Get Out Of Debt job
GOS	Gay Or Straight
GOTDPWYD	Get Off The Damn Phone While You're Driving
GOWI	Get On With It

GOYHH	Get Off Your High Horse
GQMF	Gentleman's Quarterly Mother F***er
GR&D	Grinning Running & Ducking
GR2BR	Good Riddance To Bad Rubbish
GR8	Great
GRAS	Generally Recognized As Safe
gratz	Congratulations
GROBR	Good Riddance Of Bad Rubbish
grrlz	girls, also seen as grrl
GRRR	growling
GSC	Gimme Some Credit
GSOAS	Go Sit On A Snake
GSOH	Good Sense Of Humor
GSW	Gun Shot Wound
GSYJDWURMNKH	Good Seeing You, Just Don't Wear Your Monkey Hat
GT	Good Try
GTASC	Going To A Strip Club
GTFO	Get The F*** Out
GTFOOH	Get The F*** Out Of Here
GTG	Got To Go
GTGB	Got To Go Bye
GTGP	Got To Go Pee
GTH	Go To Hell
GTK	Good To Know
GTM	Giggle To Myself
GTRM	Going To Read Mail
GTS	Google That Sh**
GTSY	Glad To See You
GUD	Geographically UnDesirable
guvment, guvmint	government, also seen as gumint

GWI	Get With It
GWOT	Glorified Waste Of Time
GWS	Get Well Soon
GYHOOYA	Get Your Head Out Of Your Ass
GYPO	Get Your Pants Off

_____
_____
_____
_____
_____
_____
_____
_____
_____
_____
_____
_____
_____
_____
_____
_____
_____
_____
_____
_____
_____
_____

-H-

H&K	Hugs and Kisses
h/o	Hold On
h/p	Hold Please
H2CUS	Hope To See You Soon
H2S	Here To Stay
H4U	Hot For You
H4XX0R	Hacker -or- To Be Hacked
H9	Husband in room
HADVD	Have Advised
hag1	have a good one
HAGD	Have a Great Day
HAGN	Have A Good Night
HAGO	Have A Good One
hahaha	it means laughing
HAK	Hugs And Kisses
HAND	Have a Nice Day
HAR	Hit And Run
HAWTLW	Hello And Welcome To Last Week
HAY	How Are You?
HB	Hurry Back
HBASTD	Hitting Bottom And Starting To Dig
HBB	Hip Beyond Belief
HBIB	Hot But Inappropriate Boy
HBIC	Head Bitch In Charge
HBO	Helping a Brother Out
HBTU	Happy Birthday To You
HBU	How Bout You?
HCC	Holy Computer Crap

HD	Hold
HDGFS	How Does Get F***ed Sound?
HF	Hello Friend -or- Have Fun -or- Have Faith
HHFO	Hell Has Frozen Over
HHH	Hip Hip Hooray
HHIS	Hanging Head In Shame
HHO1/2K	Ha Ha, Only Half Kidding
HHOJ	Ha Ha, Only Joking
HHOK	Ha Ha, Only Kidding
HHOS	Ha Ha, Only Serious
HHTYAY	Happy Holidays To You And Yours
Hi 5	High Five
HIG	How's It Going?
HIH	Hope It Helps
HIOOC	Help, I'm Out Of Coffee
HITAKS	Hang In There And Keep Smiling
HMFIC	Head MOFO In Charge
HMU	Hit Me Up
HNTI	How Nice That/This Is
HNTW	How Nice That Was
HNY	Happy New Year
HO	Hang On -or- Hold On
HOHA	HOllywood HAcker
HOIC	Hold On, I'm Coming
HOT PIC	Hot Picture, as in sexy or naked
howru	How Are You
HOYEW	Hanging On Your Every Word
HP	Higher Power
HPOA	Hot Piece Of Ass
HPPO	Highest Paid Person in Office

HRCN	it means hurricane
HSIAB	Haven't Seen It All Before
HSIK	How Should I Know
HT	Hi There -or- Hat Tip
HTB	Hang The Bastards
HTH	Hope This (or That) Helps
HTNOTH	Hit The Nail On The Head
HU	Hook Up
HUA	Heads Up Ace -or- Head Up Ass -or- Heard, Understood, Acknowledged
HUD	How You Doing?
HUGZ	Hugs
huh	what
HUYA	Head Up Your Ass
HV	Have
HWGA	Here We Go Again
hx	it means history -or- hospital

_____
_____
_____
_____
_____
_____
_____
_____
_____
_____
_____
_____

-I-

I 1-D-R	I Wonder
I <3 I	I Love It
I <3 U	I Love You
i h8 it	i hate it
I&I	Intercourse & Inebriation
I-D-L	Ideal
IAC	In Any Case -or- I Am Confused -or- If Anyone Cares
IAE	In Any Event
IAGTKOM	I Ain't Got That Kind Of Money
IAITS	It's All In The Subject
IANAC	I Am Not A Crook
IANADBIPOOTV	I Am Not A Doctor But I Play One On TV
IANAE	I Am Not An Expert
IANAL	I Am Not A Lawyer
IANNNGC	I Am Not Nurturing the Next Generation of Casualties
IASAP4U	I Always Say A Prayer For You
IAT	I Am Tired
IAW	I Agree With -or- In Accordance With
IAYM	I Am Your Master
IBGYBG	I'll Be Gone, You'll Be Gone
IBIWISI	I'll Believe It When I See It
IBK	Idiot Behind Keyboard
IBRB	I'll Be Right Back
IBT	In Between Technology
IBTC	Itty Bitty Titty Committee
IBTD	I Beg To Differ

IBTL	In Before The Lock
IC	Independant Contractor -or- In Character -or- I See
ICBW	I Could Be Wrong
ICBWICBM	It Could Be Worse, It Could Be Me
ICCL	I Couldn't Care Less
ICIHICPCL	I Can't Imagine How I Could Possibly Care Less
ICW	I Can't Wait
ICWUM	I See What You Mean
ICYC	In Case You're Curious -or- In Case You Care
ICYMI	In Case You Missed It
ID	IDentification
ID10T	Idiot
IDC	I Don't Care
IDGAD	I Don't Give A Damn
IDGAF	I Don't Give A F***
IDGARA	I Don't Give A Rats Ass
IDGI	I Don't Get It -or- I Don't Get Involved
IDIFTL	I Did It For The Lulz
IDK	I Don't Know
IDK, my BFF Jill	I Don't Know, my Best Friend Forever Jill
IDKABTT	I Don't Know About That
IDKY	I Don't Know You
IDM	It Doesn't Matter
IDRK	I Don't Really Know
IDST	I Didn't Say That
IDTA	I Did That Already
IDTBBF	I Deserve To Be Blown First
IDTS	I Don't Think So

IDWTUB	I Don't Want To Upset You But
IEF	It's Esther's Fault
IF/IB	In the Front -or- In the Back
IFAB	I Found A Bug
IFH8TABX	I F***ing Hate This Acronym Bollocks
IFU	I F***ed Up
IGGP	I Gotta Go Pee
IGTP	I Get The Point
IGWS	It Goes Without Saying
IGWST	It Goes Without Saying That
IGYHTBT	I Guess You Had To Be There
IHA	I Hate Acronyms
IHAIM	I Have Another Instant Message
IHNC	I Have No Clue
IHNO	I Have No Opinion
IHTFP	I Have Truly Found Paradise -or- I Hate This F***ing Place
IHU	I Hear You
IHY	I Heart You -or- I Hate You
IIABDFI	If It Ain't Broke, Don't Fix It
IIIO	Intel Inside, Idiot Outside
IIMAD	If It Makes Any Difference
IINM	If I'm Not Mistaken
IIR	If I Remember -or- If I Recall
IIRC	If I Remember / Recall Correctly
IIT	Is It Tight?
IITLYTO	If It's Too Loud You're Too Old
IITM	It's In The Mail
IITYWIMWYBMAD	If I Tell You What It Means Will You Buy Me A Drink
IITYWYBMAD	If I Tell You Will You Buy Me A Drink

IIWII	It Is What It Is
IIWM	If It Were Me
IJ	Inside Joke
IJPMP	I Just Pissed My Pants
IJS	I'm Just Saying...
IJWTK	I Just Want To Know
IJWTS	I Just Want To Say
IKALOPLT	I Know A Lot Of People Like That
IKR	I Know, Right?
IKWYM	I Know What You Mean
IKYABWAI	I Know You Are But What Am I
ILA	I Love Acronyms
ILF/MD	I Love Female/Male Dominance
ILI	I Love It
ILICISCOMK	I Laughed, I Cried, I Spat/Spilt Coffee/Crumbs/Coke On My Keyboard
ILMJ	I Love My Job
ILU	I Love You
ILUAAF	I Love You As A Friend
ILY	I Love You
ILY2	I Like/Love You Too
IM	Instant Messaging -or- Immediate Message
IM2BZ2P	I aM Too Busy To (even) Pee
IMA	I Might Add
IMAO	In My Arrogant Opinion
IMCO	In My Considered Opinion
IME	In My Experience
IMEZRU	I Am Easy, Are You?
IMFAO	In My F***ing Arrogant Opinion
imfkd^	I am f***ed up
IMGC	I Might Get Caught

IMHEIUO	In My High Exalted Informed Unassailable Opinion
IMHIF	I Move How I Feel
IMHO	In My Humble Opinion
IMI	I Mean It
IMJS	I'M Just Saying
IMML	I Make Myself Laugh
IMNERHO	In My Never Even Remotely Humble Opinion
IMNSHO	In My Not So Humble Opinion
IMO	In My Opinion
IMOO	In My Own Opinion
IMOWHA	I Made Out With Him/Her Anyway
IMPOV	In My Point Of View
IMR	I Mean Really
IMRU	I Am, Are You?
IMS	I Am Sorry
INBD	It's No Big Deal
INMP	It's Not My Problem
INNW	If Not Now When?
INPO	In No Particular Order
INUCOSM	It's No Use Crying Over Spilt Milk
IOH	I'm Outta Here
ION	Index Of Names
IONO	I Don't Know
IOT	In Order To
IOTTCO	Intuitively Obvious To The Casual Observer
IOU	I Owe You
IOU	DInside, Outside, Upside Down
IOW	In Other Words
IPN	I'm Posting Naked

IRL	In Real Life
IRNCOT	I'd Rather Not Comment On That
ISAGN	I See A Great Need
ISH	Insert Sarcasm Here
ISO	In Search Of
ISS	I Said So -or- I'm So Sure
ISSOYS	I'm So Sick Of Your Sh**/ Stuff / Stories
ISSYGTI	I'm So Sure You Get The Idea
ISTM	It Seems To Me
ISTR	I Seem To Remember
ISWC	If Stupid Were a Crime
ISWYM	I See What You Mean
ISYALS	I'll Send You A Letter Soon
ITA	I Totally Agree
ITFA	In The Final Analysis
ITIGBS	I Think I'm Going To Be Sick
ITM	In The Money
ITMA	It's That Man Again
ITS	Intense Text Sex
ITS A D8	It's A Date
ITSFWI	If The Shoe Fits Wear It
IUM	If You Must
IUR	IIf You Are Interested
IWALU	I Will Always Love You
IWBAPTAKYAIYSTA	I Will Buy A Plane Ticket And Kick Your Ass If You Say That Again
IWBNI	It Would Be Nice If
IWFU	I Wanna F*** You
IWIWU	I Wish I Was You
IWSN	I Want Sex Now
IYAM	If You Ask Me

IYAOYAS	If You Ain't Ordinance You Ain't Sh**
IYCSSNASDSAAA	If You Can't Say Something Nice About Someone Don't Say Anything At All
IYD	In Your Dreams
IYDMMA	If You Don't Mind My Asking
IYFD	In Your F***ing Dreams
IYFEG	Insert Your Favorite Ethnic Group
IYKWIM	If You Know What I Mean
IYKWIMAITYD	If You Know What I Mean And I Think You Do
IYNAEGBTM	If You Need Anything Else Get Back To Me
IYO	In Your Opinion
IYQ	I Like You
IYSS	If You Say So
IYSWIM	If You See What I Mean

-J-

J/C	Just Checking
J/J	Just Joking
J/K	Just Kidding
J/O	Jerking Off
J/P	Just Playing
J/W	Just Wondering
J2LYK	Just To Let You Know
J4F	Just For Fun
J4G	Just For Grins
J4T or JFT	Just For Today
J5M	Just Five Minutes
JAD	Just Another Day
JAFO	Just Another F***ing Onlooker
JAFS	Just A F***ing Salesman
JAM	Just A Minute
JAS	Just A Second
JC	Just Curious -or- Just Chilling -or- Jesus Christ
JDI	Just Do It
JDMJ	Just Doing My Job
Jealz	Jealous
JEOMK	Just Ejaculated On My Keyboard
JFH	Just F*** Her
JFI	Just For Information
JGMB	Just Google Me B*tch
JHO	Just Helping Out
JHOM_	Just Helping out My Mafia / Mob / Neighbors, etc.

JHOMF	Just Helping Out My Friend(s)
JIC	Just In Case
JK	Just Kidding
JM2C	Just My 2 Cents
JMO	Just My Opinion
JOML	Jesus On the Main Line
JOOTT	Just One Of Those Things
JP	Just Playing
JSU	Just Shut Up
JSYK	Just So You Know
JT	Just Teasing
JTLYK	Just To Let You Know
JTOL	Just Thinking Out Loud
JTOU	Just Thinking Of You
JUADLAM	Jumping Up And Down Like A Monkey
JW	Just Wondering

-K-

K	OK
KAB	Kick Ass Bitch
KB	Kick Butt
KBD	Keyboard
KC	Keep Cool
KCCO	Keep Calm & Carry On
kewl	it means cool
KFY -or- K4Y	Kiss For You
KHYF	Know How You Feel
KIA	Killed In Action
KIBO	Knowledge In, Bullsh** Out
KIPPERS	Kids In Parents' Pockets Eroding Retirement Savings
KIR	Keep It Real
KISS	Keep It Simple Stupid
KIT	Keep In Touch
kitty	it means pussy
KITY	Keep It To Yourself
KK	Kiss Kiss -or- OK
KKK	over, as in, waiting for your reply
KMA	Kiss My Ass
KMBA	Kiss My Black Ass
KMFHA	Kiss My Fat Hairy Ass
KMIM	Keep Me In Mind
KMP	Keep Me Posted
KMRIA	Kiss My Royal Irish Arse
KMSLA	Kiss My Shiny Little Ass
KMUF	Kiss Me You Fool

KMWA	Kiss My White Ass
KO	Knocked Out
KOK	Knock
KOTC	Kiss On The Cheek
KOTL	Kiss On The Lips
KPC	Keeping Parents Clueless
KS	Kill Stealer
kudt	Dutch for f***ed up life
KUTGW	Keep Up The Good Work
KWIM	Know What I Mean?
KWSTA	Kiss With Serious Tongue Action
KYBC	Keep Your Bum Clean
KYFC	Keep Your Fingers Crossed
KYNC	Keep Your Nose Clean
KYPO	Keep Your Pants On
KYSOTI	Keep Your Stick On The Ice

-L-

L	Laugh
L&R	Love and Respect
L/M	Left Message
L8R	Later
L?^	Let's hook up
L@U	Laughing At / About You
LABATYD	Life's A Bitch And Then You Die
LAFW	Listening (but) Away From Window
LAGNAF	Lets All Get Naked And F***
LAOJ	Laughing At Own Joke
LAQ	Lame Ass Quote
LB?W/C	Like Bondage? Whips or Chains
LBH	Let's Be Honest
LBR and LGR	Little Boy's Room and Little Girl's Room
LBS	Laughing But Serious
LBUG or LBIG	Laughing Because You're Gay -or- Laughing Because I'm Gay
LD	Long Distance -or- Later Dude
LDIMEDILLIGAF	Look Deeply Into My Eyes, Does It Look Like I Give A F***
LDR	Long Distance Relationship
LDTTWA	Let's Do The Time Warp Again
LF	Let's F***
LFTI	Looking Forward To It
LFU	Life"s F***ed Up
LG	Life's Good -or- Long Gone
LGBT	Lesbian, Gay, Bisexual, Transgender
LGMAS	Lord Give Me A Sign

LH	Laughing Hysterically
LH6	Let's Have Sex
LHK	Love Hugs Kisses
LHM	Lord Have Mercy
LHO	Laughing Head Off
LHO	SLets Have Online Sex
LHSO	Let's Have Sex Online
LHU	Let's Hook Up
LIB	Lying In Bed
LIFO	Last In, First Out
LIG	Let It Go
LIR	Let It Rest
LIS	Laughing In Silence
LJBF	Let's Just Be Friends
LKITR	Little Kid In The Room
LLL	ivin' Large
LLAP	Live Long and Prosper
LLOM	Like Leno on Meth
LLT	Looks Like Trouble
LLTA	Lots and Lots of Thunderous Applause
LM46	Let's Meet For Sex
LM4a~##zzzz>	Let's Meet For A Joint
LMAO	Laughing My Ass Off
LMBAO	Laughing My Black Ass Off
LMBPO	Laughing My Booty Pop Off
LMFAO	Laughing My F***ing Ass Off
LMHO	Laughing My Head Off
LMIRL	Let's Meet In Real Life
LMK	Let Me Know
LMKHTWOFY	Let Me Know How That Works Out For Yo

LMOA	Left a Message On your Answering machine
LMP	Lick My Pussy
LMS	Like My Status
LMSO	Laughing My Socks Off
LMTA	Like Minds Think Alike
LMTC	Left a Message To Contact
LMTCB	Left Message To Call Back
lo	it means hello
LOB	Lying On Bed
LOK	Lots Of Kisses
LOL	Laughing Out Loud -or- Lots Of Love -or- Living On Lipitor
LOL WUSS	Laugh Out Loud With Unintentional Snort Sound
LOLA	Laugh Out Loud Again
LOLPMP	Laugh Out Loud Peed My Pants
LOLROTF&ICGU	Laughing Out Loud Rolling On The Floor & I Can't Get Up
LOLZ	Lots Of Laughs
LOMBARD	Lots Of Money But A Right Dick
LOML	Love Of My Life
LONH	Lights On, Nobody Home
LOOL	Laughing Outrageously Out Loud
LOOMM	Laughing Out Of My Mind
LOPSOD	Long On Promises, Short On Delivery
LORE	Learn Once, Repeat Everywhere
LOU	Laughing Over You
LOVE	Lots Of Voluntary Effort
LPC	Lead Pipe Cinch
LPOS	Lazy Piece Of Sh**

LRF	Little Rubber Feet
LSB	Life Sucks Balls
LSHITIPAL	Laughing So Hard I Think I Peed A Little
LSHMBH	Laughing So Hard My Belly Hurts
LSV	Language, Sex, Violence
LTF	Lick The Floor
LTHTT	Laughing Too Hard To Type
LTIC	Laughing 'Til I Cry
LTIO	Laughing Til I Orgasm
LTM	Laughing To Myself
LTNS	Long Time No See
LTNT	Long Time, No Type
LTR	Long Term Relationship
LTS	Laughing to Self
LTTIC	Look The Teacher Is Coming
LuK	it means good luck
LULU	Locally Undesireable Land Use
lulz	laughs or LulzSec
LUMTP	Love You More Than Pie
LUMU	Love You Miss You
LUMUMI	Love You Miss You Mean It
luser	loser
LUSM	Love You So Much
luv	it means love
LWR	Launch When Ready
LWU	Laughing With You
LWYS	Look What You Started
LY	Love You
LY4E	Love You Forever
LYA	Love You All
LYB	Love You Babe

LYCYLBB	Love You, See You Later, Bye Bye
LYKYAMY	Love You, Kiss You, Already Miss You
LYL	Love You Lots
LYLAB	Love You Like a Brother
LYLAS	Love You Like A Sister
LYLB	Love You Later Bye
LYMI	Love You, Mean It
LYSOUAQ	Learn Your Sh** Or Up And Quit
LYSYB	Love Ya, See Ya, Bye
LYWAMH	Love You With All My Heart

_____
_____
_____
_____
_____
_____
_____
_____
_____
_____
_____
_____
_____
_____
_____
_____
_____
_____
_____
_____

-M-

M	Mom
M2NY	Me Too, Not Yet
M4C	Meet for Coffee
M4M	Men for Men -or- Male for Male
m4w	men for women
M8 or M8s	Mate -or- Mates
MA	Mature Audience
MAYA	Most Advanced Yet Accessible
MB	Message Board
MBN	Must Be Nice
MBRFN	Must Be Real F***ing Nice
MCM	Man Crush Monday
MD	Doctor of Medicine -or- Managing Director
MDR	Mort De Rire
MEGO	My Eyes Glaze Over
meh	Who cares, whatever
MEJR	My Eyes Just Rolled
MF	My Friend
MFD	Multi-Function Device
MfG	Mit freundlichen Gruessen
MFIC	Mother F***er In Charge
MFRC	My Fingers Are Crossed
MFWIC	Mother F***er Who's In Charge
MHBFY	My Heart Bleeds For You
mhhm	uh huh -or- yeah
MHOTY	My Hat's Off To You
MHYF	Move How You Feel
MIA	Missing In Action

MIH	Make It Happen
MIHAP	May I Have Your Attention Please
MIL	Mother-In-Law
MILF	Mother I'd Like to F***
MINS	Minutes
MIRL	Meet In Real Life
MITIN	More Info Than I Needed
MKOP	My Kind Of Place
MLA	Multiple Letter Acronym
MLAS	My Lips Are Sealed
mlmg	iving the digital middle finger
MM	Market Maker -or- Merry Meet
MMHA2U	My Most Humble Apologies To You
mmk	mmm ok
MML	Made Me Laugh
MMYT	Mail Me Your Thoughts
MO	Move On
mob	it means mobile
MOF	Matter Of Fact
MOFO	Mother F***er
MOMPL	MOMent PLease
MOO	Mud Object-Oriented -or- Matter Of Opinion -or- My Opinion Only
MOOC	Massive Open Online Course
MOOS	Member Of The Opposite Sex
MOP	MOment Please
MorF	Male or Female
MOS	Mom Over Shoulder
MOSS	Member(s) Of The Same Sex
MOTAS	Member Of The Appropriate Sex
MOTD	Message Of The Day

MOTOS	Member(s) Of The Opposite Sex
MOTSS	Member(s) Of The Same Sex
MPFB	My Personal F*** Buddy
MRA	Moving Right Along
MRM	Men's Rights Movement
MRPH	Mail the Right Place for Help
MSG	Message
MSMD	Monkey See Monkey Do
MSNUW	Mini-Skirt No UnderWear
MSTA	Must See To Appreciate
MSTM	Makes Sense To Me
MT	empty -or- Modified Tweet
MTBF	Mean Time Before Failure
MTF	More To Follow
MTFBWY	May The Force Be With You
MTLA	My True Love Always
MTMMFBWY	May the Mickey Mouse Force Be With You
MTSBWY	May The Schwartz Be With You
MTSITN	More Than Ships In The Night
MUAH or MWAH	the sound of a kiss
MUBAR	Messed up Beyond All Recognition
MUSL	Missing You Sh** Loads
MUSM	Miss You So Much
MVA	Motor Vehicle Accident
MVA no PI	Motor Vehicle Accident with no Personal Injury
MVA w/PI	Motor Vehicle Accident with Personal Injury
mvto	it means thank you
MWBRL	More Will Be Revealed Later
MWS	My Wife Says

MYL	Mind Your Language
MYOB	Mind Your Own Business
MYT	Meet You There

The Largest List of Chat Acronyms & Text Shorthand

-N-

N	No -or- and
N pic	Nice picture
N-A-Y-LI	n A While
N/A	Not Applicable -or- Not Affiliated
N/M	Nothing Much
N/T	No Text
N1	Nice One
N2M	Not To Mention -or- Not Too Much
N2MJCHBU	Not Too Much Just Chillin, How Bout You
NA	Nice Ass
NAB	Not A Blonde
NADT	Not A Damn Thing
NAGB	Nearly Almost A Good Bridge
NAGI	Not A Good Idea
NAK	Nursing At Keyboard
NALOPKT	Not A Lot Of People Know That
NAMAILU	Not As Much As I Love You
NASCAR	Non-Athletic Sport Centered Around Rednecks
NATC	Not A Text Conversation
natch	Naturally
NATO	No Action, Talk Only
NAVY	Never Again Volunteer Yourself
NAZ	Name, Address, Zip -or-Nasdaq
NB	Nota Bene
NB4T	Not Before Time
NBD	No Big Deal
NBFAB	Not Bad For A Beginner

NBFABS	Not Bad For A Bot Stopper
NBG	No Bloody Good
NBIF	No Basis In Fact
NBLFY	Nothing But Love For You
NBS	No Bull Sh**
NC	Nice Crib
NCG	New College Graduate
ND	No Date
NDN	Indian
ne	any
ne-wayz	anyways
ne1	anyone
ne14kfc	Anyone for KFC?
ne1er	Anyone here?
Ne2H	Need To Have
NEET	Not currently Engaged in Employment, Education, or Training
NESEC	Any Second
NEV	Neighborhood Electric Vehicle
NEWS	North, East, West, South
NFBSK	Not For British School Kids
NFC	Not Favorably Considered -or- No F***ing Chance
NFE	No F***ing Excuses
NFF	No F***ing Fair
NFG	Not F***ing Good
NFI	No F***ing Idea
NFS	Need For Sex
NFW	No F***ing Way -or- No Feasible Way
NG	New Game
NGB	Nearly Good Bridge

NGH	Not Gonna Happen
NH	Nice Hand
NHOH	Never Heard Of Him/Her
NI	Not Interested
NI4NI	An Eye For Any Eye
NICE	Nonsense In Crappy Existence
NIDL	Not Interested, DisLike
NIFOC	Nude In Front Of The Computer
NIGYYSOB	Now I've Got You, You Son Of a B*tch
NIH	Not Invented Here
NIM	No Internal Message
NIMBY	Not In My Back Yard
NIMJD	Not In My Job Description
NIMQ	Not In My Queue
NIMY	Never In A Million Years
NINO	Nothing In, Nothing Out -or- No Input, No Output
NISM	Need I Say More
NITL	Not In This Lifetime
NIYWFD	Not In Your Wildest F***ing Dreams
NJAPF	Not Just Another Pretty Face
NLL	Nice Little Lady
NLTBRO	Not Likely To Be Run Over
NM	Never Mind -or- Nothing Much -or Not Much -or- Nice Move
nm, u	not much, you?
NME	Enemy
NMH	Not Much Here
NMHJC	Not Much Here, Just Chilling
NMP	Not My Problem
NMTE	Now More Than Ever

NMU	Not Much, You?
NN	Not Now -or- Need
NNCIMINTFZ	Not Now Chief, I'm In The F ***in' Zone
NNR	Need Not Respond
nnsh	night night sweet heart
NNWW	Nudge, Nudge, Wink, Wink
NO	Not Online
no praw	no problem
no1	it means no one
NOA	Not Online Anymore
NOFI	No OFfence Intended
noob	also seen as n00b, nub, no0blet
NOS	New Old Stock -or- Not Outside Sales
NOY	Not Online Yet
NOYB	None Of Your Business
NP	No Problem -or- Nosy Parents
NQA	No Questions Asked
NQOCD	Not Quite Our Class Dear
NR	Nice Roll
NRG	Energy
NRN	No Reply Necessary
NS	Nice Set -or- No Show
NSA	No Strings Attached
NSB	Not Sure But
NSFW	Not Safe For Work
NSS	No Sh** Sherlock
NSTLC	Need Some Tender Loving Care
NTA	Not This Again
NTABOM	Now That's A Bunch Of Malarkey
NTB	Not Too Bright
NTBN	No Text Back Needed

nth	nothing
NTIM	Not That It Matters
NTIMM	Not That It Matters Much
NTK	Nice To Know
NTL	nonetheless
NTM	Not That Much
NTMU	Nice To Meet You
NTTAWWT	Not That There's Anything Wrong With That
NTW	Not To Worry
NTYMI	Now That You Mention It
NUB	New person to a site or game
NUFF	Enough
NVM	NeVer Mind
NVNG	Nothing Ventured, Nothing Gained
NW	No Way
NWAL	Nerd Without A Life
NWOT	New WithOut Tags
NWR	Not Work Related
NWT	New With Tags
NYC	Not Your Concern
NYCFS	New York City Finger Salute

_____

_____

_____

_____

_____

_____

-O-

O	Opponent -or- Over -or- Or
OAO	Over And Out
OATUS	On A Totally Unrelated Subject
OAUS	On An Unrelated Subject
OB	Obligatory
OBE	Overcome By Events
OBO	Or Best Offer
OBTW	Oh By The Way
OBX	Old Battle Axe
OC	Original Character -or- Own Character
OCD	Obsessive Compulsive Disorder
ODTAA	One Damn Thing After Another
OF	Old Fart
OFAP	Old Fart At Play
of	cof course
OG	Original Gangsta
OIC	Oh, I See
OICU812	Oh I See, You Ate One Too
OIRWIS	Oh I Remember What I Said
OK	okay -or- all correct
OL	Old Lady
OLL	OnLine Love
OLN	OnLine Netiquette
OLO	Only Laughed Once
OM	Old Man
OMB	Oh My Buddha
OMDB	Over My Dead Body
OME	Oh My Evolution

OMFG	Oh My F***ing God
OMG	Oh My God
OMIK	Open Mouth, Insert Keyboard
OML	Oh My Lord
OMMA	Oh My Aching Ass
OMW	On My Way -or- Oh My Word
OMWT	On My Way Too
ONID	Oh No I Didn't
ONNA	Oh No, Not Again
ONNTA	Oh No, Not This Again
ONUD	Oh No You Didn't
OO	Over and Out
OOAK	One Of A Kind
OOC	Out Of Character -or- Out Of Control
OOF	Out Of Facility
OOI	Out Of Interest
OOO	Out Of Office
OOS	Out Of Stock
OOT	Out Of Touch
OOTB	Out Of The Box -or- Out Of The Blue
OOTC	Obligatory On Topic Comment
OSIF	Oh Sh** I Forgot
OSINTOT	Oh Sh** I Never Thought Of That
OST	On Second Thought
OT	Off Topic
OTASOIC	Owing To A Slight Oversight In Construction
OTC	Over The Counter
OTF	On The Floor -or- On The Fone
OTH	Off The Hook
OTL	Out To Lunch

OTOH	On The Other Hand
OTP	On The Phone
OTR	On The Road
OTS	On The Scene -or- On The Spot -or- Off The Shelf
OTT	Over The Top
OTTOMH	Off The Top Of My Head
OTW	Off The Wall -or- Otherwise
OUSU	Oh You Shut Up
ova	it means over
OWTTE	Or Words To That Effect
OZ	Australia

_____
_____
_____
_____
_____
_____
_____
_____
_____
_____
_____
_____
_____
_____
_____
_____

-P-

P	Partner
P&C	Private & Confidential
P-ZA	Pizza
P/U	Pick Up
P2C2E	Process Too Complicated Too Explain
P2U4URAQTP	Peace To You For You Are A Cutie Pie
P3r50n	it means person
P911	Parent Alert
PA	Parent Alert
PAL	Parents Are Listening -or- Peace And Love
PANS	Pretty Awesome New Stuff
PAW	Parents Are Watching
PAX	Passengers
PB	Potty Break
PBB	Parent Behind Back
PBEM	Play By EMail
PBIAB	Pay Back Is A Bitch
PBJ	Peanut Butter and Jelly -or- Pretty Boy Jock
PC	Personal Computer -or- Politically Correct
PCM	Please Call Me
PCMCIA	People Can't Memorize Computer Industry Acronyms
PD	Public Domain
PDA	Personal Digital Assistant -or- Public Display of Affection
PDOMA	Pulled Directly Out Of My Ass
PDQ	Pretty Darn Quick
PDS	Please Don't Shout

PEBCAC	Problem Exists Between Chair And Computer
PEBCAK	Problem Exists Between Chair And Keyboard
PEEP	People Engaged and Empowered for Peace
peeps	people
pen15	it means penis
PFA	Pulled From Ass -or- Please Find Attached
PFC	Pretty F***ing Cold
PFM	Pure F***ing Magic
phat	Pretty Hot And Tempting
PHB	Pointy Haired Boss
PHS	Pointy Haired Stupidvisor
PIAPS	Pig In A Pant Suit
PIBKAC	Problem Is Between Keyboard And Chair
PICNIC	Problem In Chair, Not In Computer
PIF	Paid In Full
PIMP	Peeing In My Pants
PIMPL	Peeing In My Pants Laughing
PIN	Person In Need -or- Personal Identification Number
PIR	Parent In Room
PITA	Pain In The Ass
PITMEMBOAM	Peace In The Middle East My Brother Of Another Mother
pix	pictures -or- photos
PLO	Peace, Love, Out
PLOKTA	Press Lots Of Keys To Abort
PLOS	Parents Looking Over Shoulder
PLS	Please

PLU	People Like Us
PLZ	Please
PM	Personal Message -or- Private Message
PMBI	Pardon My Butting In
PMF	Pardon My French
PMFJI	Pardon Me For Jumping In
PMIGBOM	Put Mind In Gear Before Opening Mouth
PMJI	Pardon My Jumping In
PML	Pissing Myself Laughing
PMP	Peeing My Pants
PMSL	Pissed MySelf Laughing
PNATTMBTC	Pay No Attention To The Man Behind The Curtain
PNCAH	Please, No Cursing Allowed Here
PND	Possibly Not Definitely -or- Personal Navigation Device
PO	Piss Off
POAHF	Put On A Happy Face
POAK	Passed Out At Keyboard
POMS	Parent Over My Shoulder
PONA	Person Of No Account
POP	Photo On Profile, Point Of Purchase / Presence, Post Office Protocol
POS	Parent Over Shoulder -or- Piece Of Sh**
POSC	Piece Of Sh** Computer
POSSLQ	Persons of the Opposite Sex Sharing Living Quarters
POTATO	Person Over Thirty Acting Twenty One
POTS	Plain Old Telephone System -or- Pat On The Shoulder
POTUS	President of the United States

POV	Point Of View
PP	Personal Problem
PPL	People -or- Pay-Per-Lead
PPPPPPP or 7P	Prior Proper Planning Prevents Piss Poor Performance
pron	porn
PRT	Partial ReTweet -or- Party
PRW	Parents Are Watching
PS	Post Script
PSA	Public Service Announcement
PSO	Product Superior to Operator
PTH	Prime Tanning Hours
PTL	Praise The Lord
PTMM	Please Tell Me More
PTOYED	Please Turn Off Your Electronic Devices
PTP	Pardon The Pun
PTPOP	Pat The Pissed Off Primate
PU	that stinks
puter	computer
PVP	Player Versus Player
pw	password
PWAS	Prayer Wheels Are Spinning
PWCB	Person Will Call Back
PWMS	Playing With Myself
pwn	own
pwnt	owned
PWOMS	Parent Watching Over My Shoulder
PWP	Plot, What Plot?
PYFB	Pay Your F***ing Bill

-Q-

Q	Queue -or- Question
Q2C	Quick To Cum
QC	Quality Control
QFT	Quoted For Truth -or- Quit F***ing Talking
qix	it means quick
QL	Quit Laughing
QLS	reply
QOTD	Quote Of The Day
QQ	Quick Question -or- Cry More
QS	Quit Scrolling
QT	Cutie -or- Quiet
QYB	Quit Your Bitching

_____

_____

_____

_____

_____

_____

_____

_____

_____

_____

_____

_____

_____

-R-

r	are
r u da?	Are you there?
r u goin	Are you going?
r u there?	Are you there?
R&D	Research & Development
R&R	Rest & Relaxation
RAEBNC	Read And Enjoyed, But No Comment
RAF	Random As F***
RAFO	Read And Find Out
RAT	Remotely Activated Trojan -or- Remote Access Tool
RB@Ya	Right Back at Ya
RBAY	Right Back At You
RBTL	Read Between The Lines
RBU	Rainbows, Butterflies, Unicorns
RC	Remote Control
RCI	Rectal Cranial Inversion
RDV	Reader's Digest Version
RE	Regards -or- Reply -or- Hello Again
REHI	Hi Again
RESO	Reservation
RFD	Request For Discussion
RFP	Request For Proposal
RFR	Really F***ing Rich
RFS	Really F***ing Soon
rgds	it means regards
RGR	Roger
RHIP	Rank Has Its Privileges

RHK	RoundHouse Kick
RI&W	Read It And Weep
RIMJS	Really I'M Just Saying
RINO	Republican In Name Only
RIYL	Recommended If You Like
RKBA	Right to Keep and Bear Arms
RL	Real Life
RLCO	Real Life Conference
RLF	Real Life Friend
RM	Remake
RMB	Rings My Bell
RMETTH	Rolling My Eyes To The Heavens
RMLB	Read My Lips Baby
RMMA	Reading My Mind Again
RMMM	Read My Mail Man
RN	Right Now
RNN	Reply Not Necessary
RNY	it means rainy
ROFL	Rolling On Floor Laughing
ROFLMAO	Rolling On Floor Laughing My Ass Off
ROFLMAOASTC	Rolling On Floor Laughing My Ass Off And Scaring The Cat
ROFLOL	Rolling On Floor Laughing Out Loud
ROR	Raffing Out Roud (in scooby-doo dialect)
ROTFL	Rolling On The Floor Laughing
ROTFLMAO	Rolling On The Floor Laughing My Ass Off
ROTFLMFAO	Rolling On The Floor Laughing My F***ing Ass Off
ROTFLOL	Rolling On The Floor Laughing Out Loud
ROTGL	Rolling On The Ground Laughing

ROTGLMAO	Rolling On The Ground Laughing My Ass Off
ROTM	Right On The Money
RPG	Role Playing Games
RRQ	Return Receipt reQuested
RRR	haR haR haR (instead of LOL)
RSN	Real Soon Now
RSVP	Repondez S'il Vous Plait
RT	Real Time -or- ReTweet
RTB	Returning To Base
RTBM	Read The Bloody Manual
RTBS	Reason To Be Single
RTFAQ	Read The FAQ
RTFF	Read The F***ing FAQ
RTFM	Read The F***ing Manual
RTFQ	Read The F***ing Question
RTH	Release The Hounds
RTK	Return To Keyboard
RTM or RTFM	Read The Manual -or- Read The F***ing Manual
RTS	Read The Screen
RTSM	Read The Silly Manual
RTSS	Read The Screen Stupid
RTTSD	Right Thing To Say Dude
RTWFQ	Read The Whole F***ing Question
RU	Are You?
RU/18	Are You Over 18?
RUFKM	Are You F***ing Kidding Me?
RUH	Are You Horny?
RUMCYMHMD	Are You on Medication Cause You Must Have Missed a Dose

RUMORF	Are You Male OR Female?
RUNTS	Are You Nuts?
RUOK	Are You OK?
RUS	Are You Serious?
RUSOS	Are You SOS (in trouble)?
RUT	Are You There?
RUUP4IT	Are You Up For It?
RU\\18	Are You Under 18?
RX	Regards
RYFM	Read Your Friendly Manual
RYO	Roll Your Own
RYS	Read Your Screen

-S-

S	Smile
S2R	Send To Receive
S2U	Same To You
S3<==8	screwed in the ass
S4B	Sh** for Brains
S4L	Spam For Life
SADAD	Suck A Dick And Die
SAHM	Stay At Home Mom
SAIA	Stupid Asses In Action
SANM	Starting A New Message
SAPFU	Surpassing All Previous Foul Ups
SB	Stand By
SBI	Sorry 'Bout It
SBTA	Sorry, Being Thick Again
SBUG	Small Bald Unaudacious Goal
SC	Stay Cool
SCNR	Sorry, Could Not Resist
SCUICHT	So Coked Up I Can Hardly Type
SDFB	Smoke Dope F*** B*tches
SDK	Scottie Doesn't Know -or- Software Developer's Kit
sec	wait a second
SED	Said Enough Darling
SEG	Sh** Eating Grin
SEP	Somebody Else's Problem
SETE	Smiling Ear To Ear
SEWAG	Scientifically Engineered Wild Ass Guess
SEX	ALL CAPS for sex

SF	Surfer Friendly -or- Science Fiction
SFAIAA	So Far As I Am Aware
SFB	Sh** For Brains
SFETE	Smiling From Ear To Ear
SFLA	Stupid Four Letter Acronym
SFP	Sorry For Partying
SFTTM	Stop F***ing Talking To Me
SFX	Sound Effects -or- Stage Effects
SGTM	Sounds Good To Me
SH	Sh** Happens
SHB	Should Have Been
shhh	it means be quiet
SHID	Slap Head In Disgust
SHIT	Sugar Honey Ice Tea
SHMILY	See How Much I Love You
SHT	it means so hot
SHTF	Sh** Hits The Fan
SHWASLOMF	Sitting Here With A Straight Look On My Face
SIA	Say It Again
SIC	Spelling Is Correct
SICL	Sitting In Chair Laughing
SICS	Sitting In Chair Snickering
SII	Seriously Impaired Imagination
SIL	Sister-In-Law
SIN	Stop It Now
SIP	Skiing In Powder
SIT	Stay In Touch
SITCOM	Single Income, Two Children, Oppressive Mortgage
SITD	Still In The Dark

SITUBI	Say It Til You Believe It
SIUP	Suck It Up Pussy
SIUYA	Shove It Up Your Ass
SJ	Strong Jaws
sk8er	skater
Sknkr	Skincare
SL	Second Life
SLAP	Sounds Like A Plan
SLAW	Sounds Like A Winner
SLIRK	Smart Little Rich Kid
SLM	See Last Mail
SLOM	Sticking Leeches On Myself
SLT	Something Like That
SM	Senior Moment
sm1	it means someone
SMAIM	Send Me An Instant Message
SMAO	Sweating My Ass Off
SMB	Suck My Balls
SMD	Suck My Dick
SME	Subject Matter Expert
SMEM	Send Me E-Mail
SMH	Shaking My Head
SMIM	Send Me an Instant Message
SMOP	Small Matter of Programming
smt	something
SN	Side Note
SNAFU	Situation Normal, All F***ed Up
SNAG	Sensitive New Age Guy
SNERT	Snotty Nosed Egotistical Rotten Teenager
SNIF	Simple Nice Index File
SNNSHWRS	it means sun showers

SNNY	it means sunny
SO	Significant Other
SOB	Son Of a B*tch
SOBT	Stressed Out Big Time
SODDI	Some Other Dude Did It
SOE	Start Of Exams
SOGOP	Sh** Or Get Off the Pot
SOH	Sense Of Humor
SOHF	Sense Of Humor Failure
SOI	Self Owning Idiot
SOIAR	Sit On It And Rotate
SoIC	So I See
sok	it's ok
SOL	Sh** Out of Luck -or- Sooner Or Later
solomo	Social, Local, Mobile
some1	someone
SOMF	Sit On My Face
SOMY	Sick Of Me Yet
SOOYA	Snake Out Of Your Ass
SOP	Standard Operating Procedure
SorG	Straight or Gay
SOS	Same Old Sh** -or- help
SOSAD	Same Old Song And Dance
SOT	Short On Time
SOTMG	Short On Time, Must Go
SOW	Speaking Of Which -or- Statement Of Work
soz	Sorry
spk	it means speak
SPOC	Single Point Of Contact
SRLB	Spoiled Rotten Little Brat
SRO	Standing Room Only

srsly	seriously
sry	it means sorry
SSA	it means ass backwards
SSC	Super Sexy Cute
SSDD	Same Sh** Different Day
SSEWBA	Someday Soon, Everything Will Be Acronyms
SSIA	Subject Says It All
STBX	Soon To Be Ex
STBY	Sucks To Be You
STD	Seal The Deal, Save The Date, Sexually Transmitted Disease, Stuff To Do
STFU	Shut The F*** Up
STFW	Search The F***ing Web
sth	something
STHU	Shut The Hell Up
STM	Spank The Monkey
STML	Short Term Memory Loss
STPPYNOZGTW	Stop Picking Your Nose, Get To Work
STR8	Straight
STS	So To Speak
STST	Sweet Tea SweeTie
STW	Search The Web
STYS	Speak To You Soon
SU	Shut Up
SUAC	Sh** Up A Creek
SUAKM	Shut Up And Kiss Me
SUB	Shut Up Bitch
SUFI	Super Finger -or- Shut Up F***ing Imbecile
SUFID	Screwing Up Face In Disgust
SUL	Snooze You Lose

sup	what's up?
sux	sucks
SUYF	Shut Up You Fool
SWAG	Scientific Wild Ass Guess -or-
	SoftWare And Giveaways
SWAK	Sealed / Sent With A Kiss
SWALBCAKWS	Sealed With A Lick Because A Kiss
	Won't Stick
SWALK	Sealed With A Loving Kiss
SWDYT	So What Do You Think?
sweet<3	sweetheart
SWF	Single White Female
SWIM	See What I Mean?
SWIS	See What I'm Saying
SWIT	Sit and Sweat
SWL	Screaming With Laughter
SWMBO	She Who Must Be Obeyed
SWU	So What's Up
SxE	Straight Edge
SYK	So You Know
SYL	See You Later
SYS	See You Soon
SYT	See You Tomorrow
s^	what's up?

-T-

T&C	Terms & Conditions
t+	it means think positive
t2go	Time to Go
T2UL	Talk To You Later
T2UT	Talk To You Tomorrow
T@YL	Talk At You Later
TA	Thanks Again
TABOM	That's A Bunch Of Malarkey
TABOOMA	Take A Bite Out Of My Ass
TAF	That's All, Folks
TAFN	That's All For Now
TAH	Take A Hike
TAHITMOTS	There's A Hole In The Middle Of The Sea
TAKS	That's A Knee Slapper
TAM	Thanks A Million
TANJ	There Ain't No Justice
TANSIT	There's A New Sheriff In Town
TANSTAAFL	There Ain't No Such Thing As A Free Lunch
TAP	Take A Pill
TARFU	Things Are Really F***ed Up
TAS	Taking A Shower
TAW	Teachers Are Watching
TAYN	Thinking About You Now
TB	Titty Bar
TBA	To Be Advised
TBC	To Be Continued
TBD	To Be Determined
TBE	Thick Between Ears

TBH	To Be Honest
TBIU	The Bitch Is Ugly
TBT	Throwback Thursday
TBU	Thinking 'Bout You
TBYB	Try Before You Buy
TC	Take Care
TCB	Trouble Came Back -or- Taking Care of Business
TCOB	Taking Care Of Business
TCOYT	ake Care Of Yourself
TD&H	Tall, Dark and Handsome
TDM	Too Darn Many
TDTM	Talk Dirty To Me
TEOTWAWKI	The End Of The World As We Know It
TF	Too Funny
TFDS	That's For Darn Sure
TFH	Thread From Hell
TFLMS	Thanks For Letting Me Share
TFM	Thanks From Me
TFMIU	The F***ing Manual Is Unreadable
TFN	Thanks For Nothing -or- Til Further Notice
TFS	Thanks For Sharing -or- Three Finger Salut
TFTC	Thanks For The Cache
TFTHAOT	Thanks For The Help Ahead Of Time
TFTT	Thanks For The Thought
TFTU	Thanks For The Update
TFX	Traffic
TFYS	The F*** You Say
TG4A	Thank God For Acronyms
TGAL	Think Globally, Act Locally
TGGTG	That Girl/Guy has Got To Go

TGIF	Thank God It's Friday
THX or TX or THKS	Thanks
TIA	Thanks In Advance
TIAIL	Think I Am In Love
TIC	Tongue In Cheek
TIGAS	Think I Give A Sh**
TILF	Teacher I'd Like to F***
TILII	Tell It Like It Is
TIME	Tears In My Eyes
TINGTES	There Is No Gravity, The Earth Sucks
TINWIS	That Is Not What I Said
TISC	This Is So Cool
TISL	This Is So Lame
TISNC	This Is So Not Cool
TISNF	That Is So Not Fair
TISNT	That Is So Not True
TJBNJ	This Job Beats No Job
TK	To Come
TKO	Technical Knock Out
TKU4UK	Thank You For Your Kindness
tl;dr	too long; didn't read
TLA	Three Letter Acronym
TLC	Tender Loving Care
TLGO	The List Goes On
TLITBC	That's Life In The Big City
TLK2UL8R	Talk To You Later
TM	Trust Me
TMA	Too Many Acronyms
TMALSS	To Make A Long Story Short
TMI	Too Much Information
TMSAISTI	That's My Story And I'm Sticking To It

TMSGO	Too Much Sh** Going On
TMTOWTDI	There's More Than One Way To Do It
TNA	Temporarily Not Available
TNC	Tongue In Cheek
TNT	Til Next Time
TNTL	Trying Not To Laugh
TNX	Thanks
to go nookleer	to explode
TOBAL	There Oughta Be A Law
TOBG	This Oughta Be Good
TOM	Tomorrow
TOMTB	Taking Off My Training Bra
TOON	short for cartoon
TOPCA	Til Our Paths Cross Again
TOT	Tons Of Time
TOY	Thinking Of You
TP	Team Player -or- TelePort -or- Thanks Pal -or- Toilet Paper
TPC	The Phone Company
TPIYP	To Put In Your Prayers
TPS	That's Pretty Stupid
TPT	Trailor Park Trash
TPTB	The Powers That Be
TQM	Total Quality Management
TRAM	The Rest Are Mine
TRDMC	Tears Running Down My Cheeks
tripdub	it means www
TRNDO	it means tornado
troo	true
TRP	Television Rating Points
TS	Tough Sh** -or- Totally Stinks

TSB	Tall, Sexy, Beautiful
TSH	Too Stinkin' Hot
TSIA	This Says It All
TSIF	Thank Science It's Friday
TSNF	That's So Not Fair
TSOB	Tough Son Of a B*tch
TSR	Totally Stuck in RAM -or- Totally Stupid Rules
TSRA	Two Shakes of a Rat's Ass
TSTB	The Sooner, The Better
TT	Big Tease
TTA	Tap That Ass
TTBOMK	To The Best Of My Knowledge
TTFN	Ta Ta For Now
TTG	Time to Go
TTIOT	The Truth Is Out There
TTKSF	Trying To Keep a Straight Face
TTMF	Ta Ta MOFO
TTS	Text To Speech
TTT	That's The Ticket -or- To The Top -or- Thought That Too
TTTH	Talk To The Hand
TTTHTFAL	Talk To The Hand The Face Ain't Listening
TTTKA	Time To Totally Kick Ass
TTTT	To Tell The Truth
TTUL	Talk To You Later
TTYAWFN	Talk To You A While From Now
TTYIAF	Talk / Type To You In A Few
TTYL	Talk / Type To You Later
TTYL8R	Talk To You Later
TTYOB	Tend To Your Own Business

TTYS	Talk To You Soon
TTYT	Talk To You Tomorrow
TU	Toes Up, as in dead
TVM4YEM	Thank You Very Much For Your E-Mail
TWD	Texting While Driving
TWHAB	This Won't Hurt A Bit
TWHE	The Walls Have Ears
TWIMC	To Whom It May Concern
TWIT	That's What I Thought
TWITA	That's What I'm Talking About
TWIWI	That Was Interesting, Wasn't It?
TWSS	That's What She Said
TWTR	Twitter
TWU	That's What's Up
TXS	Thanks
TXT	Text
TXT IM	Text Instant Message
TXT MSG	text message
TY	Thank You
TYCLO	Turn Your CAPS LOCK Off
TYG	There You Go -or- Thank You God
TYL	Text You Later -or- Thank You Lord
TYVM	Thank You Very Much

_____

_____

_____

_____

_____

_____

_____

-U-

u	You
u up	You up?
U-L	You Will
U2	You Too
u4e	Yours ForEver
u8	You ate?
UBS	Unique Buying State
UCWAP	Up a Creek Without A Paddle
UDH82BME	You'd Hate To Be Me
UDM	You're the Man
UFN	Until Further Notice
UFUF	You F***, You Fix
UG2BK	You've Got To Be Kidding
UGC	User-Generated Content
UGFSU	Your Girlfriend's Ugly
UGTR	You Got That Right
UNF	Universal Noise of Fucking
UNOIT	You Know It
unPC	unPolitically Correct
UNT	Until Next Time
UNTCO	You Need To Chill Out
UOK	Are you OK?
UPOD	Under Promise Over Deliver
ur	you are
UR2K	You Are Too Kind
URAPITA	You Are A Pain In The Ass
URSAI	You Are Such An Idiot
URW	You Are Welcome

URWS	You Are Wise
URYY4M	You Are Too Wise For Me
URZ	yours
USC	Up Sh** Creek
USCWAP	Up Sh** Creek Without A Paddle
USP	Unique Selling Proposition
UTM	You Tell Me
UV	Unpleasant Visual
UWIWU	You Wish I Was You
UWM	You Want Me
UX	User eXperience

-V-

V	Very
VBG	Very Big Grin
VBMG	Very Big Mischievous Grin
VBS	Very Big Smile
VC	Venture Capital
VCDA	Vaya Con Dios, Amigo
VEG	Very Evil Grin
VFM	Value For Money
VGN	Vegan -or- Vegetarian
VIM	Very Important Member
VIP	Very Important Person
VIV	Very Important Visitor
VM	Voice Mail
VRBS	Virtual Reality Bull Sh**
VSF	Very Sad Face
VWD	Very Well Done
VWP	Very Well Played

_____

_____

_____

_____

_____

_____

_____

_____

_____

_____

-W-

W	With -or- Working
w wult	what would you like to talk about
w's^	what's up?
W/	With
W/E	Weekend
W/O	Without
w/r/t	with regard to
w00t	We Own the Other Team
w4m	women for men
W8	Wait
W9	Wife in room
W@	What
WABI	What A Bright Idea
WABOC	What A Bunch Of Crap
WABOM	What A Bunch Of Malarkey
WACI	What A Cool Idea
WAD	Without A Doubt
WADI	What A Dumb Idea
WADR	With All Due Respect
WAEF	When All Else Fails
WAFB	What A F***ing Bitch
WAFM	What A F***ing Mess
WAFS	Warm And Fuzzies
WAFU	What A F*** Up
WAG	Wild Ass Guess
WAI	What An Idiot
WAK	What A Kiss
WAMBAM	Web Application Meets Brick And Mortar

wan2	it means want to
WAS	What A Slut
WATI	What A Terrible Idea
WAW	Waiter/Actor/Webmaster -or- What A Whore
WAWI	What A Wonderful Idea
WAYD	What Are You Doing?
WAYN	Where Are You Now?
WB	Welcome Back -or- Write Back
WBS	Write Back Soon
WBU	What 'Bout You?
WC	Who Cares -or- Water Closet
WCA	Who Cares Anyway
wckd	it means wicked
WCMTSU	We Can't Make This Sh** Up
WCW	Woman Crush Wednesday
WD	Well Done
WDALYIC	Who Died And Left You In Charge?
WDDD	Woopie Doo Da Dey
WDR	With Due Respect
WDT	Who Does That?
WDYM	What Do You Mean?
WDYMBT	What Do You Mean By That?
WDYS	What Did You Say?
WDYT	What Do You Think?
WE	Whatever
WEG	Wicked Evil Grin
wenja	it means when do you
werja	it means where do you
werru	it means where are you
werubn	it means where have you been

WETSU	We Eat This Sh** Up
WF	Way Fun
WFM	Works For Me
WG	Wicked Grin
WGAFF	Who Gives A Flying F***
WGMGD	What Get's Measured Get's Done
WHYDTM	What Have You Done To Me?
WIBAMU	Well, I'll Be A Monkey's Uncle
WIBNI	Wouldn't It Be Nice If
WIIFM	What's In It For Me
WIIFY	What's In It For You
WIIWII	Well It Is What It Is
WILB	Workplace Internet Leisure Browsing
WILCO	Will Comply
WIM	Woe Is Me
WIP	Work In Process
wirld	world
WISP	Winning Is So Pleasureable
WIT	Wordsmith In Training
WITFITS	What In The F*** Is This Sh**
WITW	What In The World
WIU	Wrap It Up
wk	it means week
wkewl	way cool
wknd	it means weekend
WLMIRL	Would Like to Meet In Real Life
WLU	Wicked, Love You
WLU2	Wicked, Love You Too
WMHGB	Where Many Have Gone Before
WMMOWS	Wash My Mouth Out With Soap
WMPL	Wet My Pants Laughing

WNDY	it means windy
WNOHGB	Where No One Has Gone Before
WO	A Work Of Art
WOG	Wise Old Guy
WOM	Word Of Mouth -or- Word Of Mouse
WOMBAT	Waste Of Money, Brains And Time
WOOF	Well Off Older Folks
woot	We Own the Other Team
WOP	With Out Papers
word	t means cool, a.k.a. word up
WOT	Waste Of Time or- it means what
WOTAM	Waste Of Time And Money
WOTD	Word Of The Day
WP	Well Played
WRM	it means warm
WRT	With Regard To -or- With Respect To
wru	Where are you?
WRUD	What Are You Doing?
WRUDATM	What Are You Doing At The Moment?
WSU	What Say You?
WT	Without Thinking -or- What The -or- Who The
WTB	Want To Buy
WTDB	What's The Difference Between
WTF	What The F***
WTFDYJS	What The F*** Did You Just Say?
WTFGDA	Way To F***ing Go, Dumb Ass
WTFH	What The F***ing Hell
WTFWYCM	Why The F*** Would You Call Me?
WTFYTT	Who The F*** You Talking To
WTG	Way To Go

WTG4a\\%/	Want To Go For A Drink
WTGP	Want To Go Private?
WTH	What The Heck
WTHIN	What The Hell Is Next
WTHOW	White Trash Headline Of the Week
WTMC	What The Mother C***
WTMI	Way Too Much Information
WTN	What Then Now? -or- Who Then Now?
WTS	Want To Sell
WTSDS	Where The Sun Don't Shine
WTSHTF	When The Sh** Hits The Fan
WTTM	Without Thinking Too Much
WU	What's Up
WUF	Where You From
WUWH	Wish You Were Here
WUWHIMA	Wish You Were Here In My Arms
wuz	was
wuz4dina	What's for dinner?
wuzup	what's up?
WWJD	What Would Jesus Do?
WWNO	Walker Wheels Need Oil
WWSD	What Would Satan Do?
WWW	World Wide Web -or- World Wide Wait -or- What Went Wrong
WWY	Where Were You?
WX	Weather
WYCM	Will You Call Me?
WYD	What You Doing?
WYFM	Would You F*** Me?
WYGISWYPF	What You Get Is What You Pay For
WYM	What do You Mean?

wymyn	women
WYP	What's Your Problem?
WYRN	What's Your Real Name?
WYS	Whatever You Say
WYSILOB	What You See Is A Load of Bullocks
WYSIWYG	What You See Is What You Get
WYSLPG	What You See Looks Pretty Good
WYT	Whatever You Think
WYTB	Wish You The Best
WYW	Wish You Well
WYWH	Wish You Were Here

_____
_____
_____
_____
_____
_____
_____
_____
_____
_____
_____
_____
_____
_____
_____
_____
_____

-X-

X	it means times
X-I-10	Exciting
XLNT	Excellent
XME	Excuse Me
XOXO	Hugs and Kisses
XOXOZZZ	Hugs and Kisses and Sweet Dreams
XQZT	Exquisite
XTC	Ecstasy
XXCC	Kiss, Kiss, Hug, Hug

_____

_____

_____

_____

_____

_____

_____

_____

_____

_____

_____

_____

_____

_____

_____

_____

_____

_____

-Y-

Y	Why? -or- Yes
YA	Yet Another -or- You -or- Your
YA yaya	Yet Another Ya-Ya (as in yo-yo)
YABA	Yet Another Bloody Acronym
YACC	Yet Another Calendar Company
YAF	Young Angry Female
YAFIYGI	You Asked For It You Got It
YAHOO	You Always Have Other Options
YAJWD	You Ain't Just Whistling Dixie
YAOTM	Yet Another Off Topic Message
YARBWYR	You're A Right Bleed'n Wanker You Are
YATFM	You Are Too F***ing Much
YATI	You're A Total Idiot
YAUN	Yet Another Unix Nerd
YB	You B*tch
YBF	You've Been F***ed
YBS	You'll Be Sorry
YBY	Yeah Baby Yeah
YBYSA	You Bet Your Sweet Ass
YCMTSU	You Can't Make This Sh** Up
YCMU	You Crack Me Up
YCT	Your Comment To
YDKM	You Don't Know Me
YEPPIES	Young Experimenting Perfection Seekers
YF	Wife
YGBK	You Gotta Be Kidding
YGBSM	You Gotta Be Sh**ing Me
YGLT	You're Gonna Love This

YGM	You've Got Mail
YGTBK	You've Got To Be Kidding
YGWYPF	You Get What You Pay For
YHM	You Have Mail
YIC	Yours In Christ
YIU	Yes, I Understand
YIWGP	Yes, I Will Go Private
YKW	You Know What?
YKWIM	You Know What I Mean
YLH	Your Loving Husband
YLLO	You Lie Like Obama
YLW	Your Loving Wife
YM	Your Mother
YMAK	You May Already Know
YMAL	You Might Also Like
YMBKM	You Must Be Kidding Me
YMMD	You Make My Day -or- You Made My Day
YMMV	Your Mileage May Vary
YMYBNYCSII	You Made Your Bed Now You Can Sleep In It
YNGBT	You're Not Gonna Believe This
YNK	You Never Know
YOLO	You Only Live Once
YOYO	You're On Your Own
YR	Yeah Right -or- you -or- your
YRYOCC	You're Running on Your Own Cookoo Clock
YS	You Stinker
YSAN	You're Such A Nerd
ysdiw8	why should i wait?
YSIC	Why Should I Care?

YSK	You Should Know
YSYD	Yeah, Sure You Do
YTB	You're The Best
YTRNW	Yeah That's Right, Now What?
YTTM	You Talk Too Much
YTTT	You Telling The Truth?
YUMPI	Young Upwardly Mobile Professional Idiot
YUPPIES	Young Urban Professionals
YVW	You're Very Welcome
YW	You're Welcome
YWIA	You're Welcome In Advance
YY4U	Too Wise For You
YYSSW	Yeah Yeah Sure Sure Whatever

-Z-

Z	it means said
zerg	To gang up on someone
ZMG or ZOMG	it means Oh My God
ZZZ	Sleeping, Bored, Tired

_____
_____
_____
_____
_____
_____
_____
_____
_____
_____
_____
_____
_____
_____
_____
_____
_____
_____
_____
_____

INTERNATIONAL TEXT TERMS

Online jargon is universal and used all over the world in text messaging, social media, email, blogs, and online postings, etc. Whatever the international word for "and" is, the symbol "&" is likely used, and the same applies to the @ sign.

Here are a few international text guidelines:
*   French sept 'seven' pronounced 'set'
    for example: k7 = cassette 'cassette'
*   German acht 'eight'
    for example: gn8 = gute Nacht 'good night'
*   Italian sei 'six' for sei 'you are'
    for example: dv6 = dove sei 'where are you'
*   Spanish dos 'two'
    for example: sl2 = saludos 'greetings'
*   Swedish ett 'one'
    for example: d1a = detta 'this'
*   Norwegian sy 'seven'
    for example: 7k = sjuk 'sick'
*   Welsh un 'one'
    for example: 1ig = unig 'only'
*   Hungarian egy 'one'
    for example: 1ik = egyik 'either'
*   Persian do 'two'
    for example: 2nya = donya 'world'

The next sections contain international language text terms including French, German, Italian, Spanish, Portuguese, Dutch, Finnish, Swedish, Welch, Czech and Chinese as seen in the book *Txtng: The Gr8 Db8* by David Crystal.

FRENCH

@+, A+, À plus - later 'later'
@2m1, a2m1 - a demain 'until tomorrow'
1 - un 'one'
12C4 - un de ces quatre 'one of these days'
2 ri 1 - de rien 'you're welcome'
6ne - cine 'cinema'
a12C4 - a un de ces quatres 'see you one of these days'
alp - a la prochaine 'bye bye for now'
amha - a mon humble avis 'in my humble opinion'
apls, @+ - a plus 'see you later'
asv - age, sexe, ville 'age sex, location'
auj - aujourd'hui 'today'
b1sur - bien sur 'of course'
bcp - beaucoup 'very much'
bi1to - bientot 'soon'
bjr - bonjour 'good day'
bsr - bonsoir 'good evening'
c, ce - c'est 'it is'
cad - c'est a dire 'that is'
cb1 - c'est bien 'that's good'
c cho - c'est chaud 'it's hot'
che - chez 'at the home of'
chu, chui, chuis - je suis 'I am'
cmal1 - c'est malin 'that's sneaky'
c pa 5pa - c'est pas sympa 'that's not nice'
cpg - c'est pas grave 'it's not bad'
ct - c'etait 'it was'
d - de 'of'
d100 - descend 'get down'

dak, d'ac - d'accord 'ok'

dqp - des que possible 'as soon as possible'

dsl - desole 'sad'

edr - ecroule de rire 'laughing out loud'

entk, entouk - en tout cas 'in any case'

fds - fin de semaine 'weekend'

ght2v1 - j'ai achete du vin 'I bought some wine'

gr - gros 'large'

GspR b1 - j'espere vien 'I hope so'

gt - j'etais 'I was'

je, g - j'ai 'I have'

je c - je sais 'I know'

je le saV - je le savais 'I knew it'

jenemar - j'en ai marre 'I'm sick of it'

je t'm - je t'aime 'I love you'

je ve, j've - je vais 'I'm going'

jms - jamais 'never'

kand, kan - quand 'when'

kdo - cadeau 'gift'

ke - que 'that, what'

kel - quell, quelle 'which'

keske - qu'est-ce que 'what'

ki - qui 'who'

koi - quoi 'what'

1ckc - elle s'est cassee 'she left'

lut, slt - salut 'hi'

mdr - mort de rire 'rolling on the floor laughing'

mr6 - merci 'thanks'

msg - message ' message'

nsp - ne sais pas 'dunno'

o - au 'in the, at the'

ok1 - aucun 'none'
oqp - occupe 'busy'
oue - ouais 'yeah'
parske - parce que 'because'
p-e, pitit - peut-etre 'maybe'
pkoi - pourquoi 'why'
po, pa - pas 'not'
qq - quelques 'some'
qqn - quelqu'un 'someone'
queske, q-c q - qu'est-ce que 'what'
koi29 - quoi de neuf 'what's new'
raf - rien a faire 'nothing to do'
ras - rien a signaler 'nothing to report'
rdv - rendez-vous 'date'
re - retour, rebonjour 'I'm back'
ril - rien 'nothing'
savapa - ca va pas 'is something wrong'
stp - s'il te plait 'please'
svp - s'il vous plait 'please'
t - t'es 'you are'
tabitou - t'habites ou 'where do you live'
tt - t'etais 'you were'
ti - petit 'little'
tjs - toujours 'always'
tkc - t'es casse 'you're tired'
tlm - tout le monde 'everyone'
t nrv - t'es enerve 'are you irritated'
tok - t'es ok 'are you ok'
toqp - t'es occupe 'are you busy'
v1 - viens 'come'
vas-y - vazi 'go'

vrman - vraiment 'really'
vx - veux 'want'
x - crois, croit 'believe'
ya - il y a 'there is/are'

_____
_____
_____
_____
_____
_____
_____
_____
_____
_____
_____
_____
_____
_____
_____
_____
_____
_____
_____
_____
_____
_____
_____

GERMAN

3n - nie niemals, mirgendwo 'no way, no how, nowhere'

3st - das war dreist 'that was cheeky'

8ung - achtung 'attention'

anws - auf nimmerwiedersehn 'for good and all'

baba - bye bye 'bye bye'

bbb - bis bald baby 'see you soon baby'

bihoba - bis hoffentlich bald 'hope to see you soon'

bild - birchen, ich liebe dich 'baby I love you'

bs - bis spater 'see you later'

dad - denk an dich 'thinking of you'

dbee - du bist ein engle 'you're an angel'

dbmtm - du bist mein traummann 'you're my dream man'

dg - dumm gelaufen 'shit happens'

DiV - Danke im Voraus 'thanks in advance'

Ff - Fortsetzung folgt 'to be continued'

G - Grinsen 'grin'

gn8 - guten nacht 'good night'

guk - gruss und kuss 'love and kisses'

G&K - Gruss und Kuss 'love and kisses'

hdal - habe dich auch lieb 'love you too'

hdl - habe dich lieb 'love you'

hdlas - hast du lust auf sex 'wanna have sex'

hdlfiue - habe dich lieb fur immer und ewig 'love you now and forever'

hdml - habe dich mega lieb 'love you lots'

HDOS - Halt die Ohren steif 'keep a stiff upper lip'

idad - ich denk an dich 'I'm thinking of you'

ild, ily - ich lieve dich 'I love you'

itvd - ich traum von dir 'I'm dreaming of you'
KA - Keine Ahnung 'no idea'
kb - korrespondenz beendet 'message ends'
kd - knuddel dich 'cuddling you'
khzm - kommste heut zu mire 'come out with me today'
KK - Kein Kommentar 'no comment'
lamito - lache mich tot 'laughing myself to death'
ldnu - lass dich nicht unterkriegen 'stand your ground'
lg - liebe grusse 'kind regards'
lidumi? - liebst du mich? 'do you love me?'
mad - mag dich 'love you'
mdt - mag dich trotzdem 'still love you'
MfG - Mit freundlichen Grussen 'with best wishes'
nok - nicht ohne kondom 'not without condom'
MWN - Meines Wissens nicht 'not to my knowledge'
Pg - Pech gehabt 'bad luck'
sofa - sonntagsfahrer 'Sunday driver'
ss - schreib zuruck 'write soon'
ssz - schreib schnell zuruck 'write back quickly'
sTn - schonen Tag noch 'have a good one'
tabu - tausend bussis 'thousand kisses'
tml - tut mir leid 'sorry'
ts - traume suss 'sweet dreams'
UAwg - Um Antwort wird gebeten 'RSVP'
wdmmg - willst du mit mir gehen 'will you come out with me'
we - wochenende 'weekend'
widmihei - wilst du mich heiraten 'will you marry me'
www - wir werden warten 'we'll wait'

ITALIAN

+- - piu o meno 'more or less'
anke - anche 'also'
c sent - ci sentiamo 'see you later'
cmq - comunque 'anyhow'
dm - domani 'tomorrow'
dp - dopo 'after'
dr - dire 'say'
dv 6 - dove sei 'where are you'
dx - destra 'right'
frs - forse 'perhaps'
ke - che 'what, that'
ki - chi 'who'
km - come 'how'
kn - con 'with'
ks - cosa 'thinkg'
-male - meno male 'luckily
mmt+ - mi manchi tantissimo 'I miss you very much'
nm - numero 'number'
nn - non 'not'
prox - prossimo 'next'
qlk - qualche 'some'
qlk1 - qualcuno 'someone'
qlks - qualcosa 'something'
qnd - quando 'when'
qndi - quindi 'therefore'
qnt - quanto 'how much'
qst - questo 'this one'
rsp - rispondi 'reply'

scs - scusa 'excuse'

sl - solo 'only'

smpr - sempre 'always'

sms - messaggio 'message'

sn - sono 'are'

spr - sapere 'know'

sw - sinistra 'left'

sxo - spero 'I hope'

t tel+trd - ti telefono piu tardi 'I'll phone you later'

trnqui - tranquillo 'calm'

trp - troppo 'too much'

tvtb - ti voglio tanto bene 'I like you very much'

xche, xke, xk - perche 'why, because'

xcio - percio 'therefore'

xo - pero 'but'

xsona - persona 'person'

xxx - tanti baci 'lots of kisses'

_____

_____

_____

_____

_____

_____

_____

_____

_____

_____

_____

SPANISH

100pre - siempre 'always'
a10 - adiós 'goodbye'
a2 - adiós 'goodbye'
aki - aquí 'here'
amr - amor 'love'
aora - ahora 'now'
asdc - al salir de clase 'after class'
asias - gracias 'thanks'
b - bien 'well, good'
bb - bebé 'baby'
bbr - bbr 'to drink'
bs, bss - besos 'kisses'
bye - adiós 'goodbye'
b7s - besitos 'kisses'
c - sé, se 'I know'
cam - cámara 'camera'
chao, chau 'adiós 'goodbye'
d - de 'from, of'
d2 - dedos 'fingers'
dcr - decir 'to say'
dew, dw - adiós 'goodbye'
dfcl - difícil 'difficult'
dim - dime 'tell me'
dnd - dónde 'where'
exo - hecho 'act'
ems - hemos 'we have'
ers - eres tú 'you are, are you'
ers2 - eres tú 'are you'

eys - ellos 'they, you'
grrr - enfadado 'angry'
finde - fin de semana 'weekend'
fsta - fiesta 'party'
hl - hasta luego 'see you later'
hla - hola 'hello'
iwal - igual 'equal'
k - que, qué 'that, what'
kbza - cabeza 'head'
kls - clase 'class'
kntm - cuéntame 'tell me'
kyat - cállate -'shut up'
KO - estoy muerto 'I'm in big trouble'
km - como 'as, like'
m1ml - mándame un mensaje luego 'send me a message later'
msj - msnsaje 'message'
mxo - mucho 'a lot'
nph - no puedo hablar 'I can't talk now'
npn - no pasa nada 'nothing's happening'
pa - para, padre 'for, father'
pco - poco 'a little'
pdt - piérdete 'get lost'
pf - por favor 'please'
pls - por favor 'please'
pq - porque, porqué 'because, why'
q - que, qu.a 'that, what'
q acs? - ¿Qué haces? 'What are you doing? '
qand, qando - cuando, cuándo 'when'
qdms - quedamos 'we're staying'
q plomo! - ¡Qué plomo! 'What a drag! '

q qrs? - ¿Qué quieres? 'What do you want? '
q risa! - ¡Qué risa! 'What a laugh! '
q sea - qué sea 'whatever'
q tal? - qué tal 'What's happening? '
sbs? - ¿sabes? 'Do you know? '
salu2 - saludos 'hello, goodbye'
sms - mensaje 'message'
spro - espero 'I hope'
tq - te quiero 'I love you'
tqi - tengo que irme 'I have to leave'
tas OK? - ¿Estás bien? 'Are you OK? '
tb - también 'also'
uni - universidad 'university, college'
vns? - ¿Vienes? 'Are you coming? '
vos - vosotros 'you'
wpa - ¡Guapa! 'Sweet! '
xdon - perdón 'sorry'
xfa - por favor 'please'
xo - pero 'but'
xq - porque, porqué 'because, why'
ymam, ymm 'llámame - call me'
zzz - dormir 'sleeping'

_____
_____
_____
_____
_____
_____

PORTUGUESE

- - - menos 'less'
+ - mais 'more'
+- - mais ou menos 'more or less'
= - igual 'equal'
bjs - beijos 'kisses'
c/ - com 'with'
c/o - como 'how'
ily ou ilu - amo-te 'i love you'
k - quê 'that, which'
lol - a rir alto 'laughing out loud'
msg - mensagem 'message'
msm - mesmo 'same'
ñ ou n ou na- não 'no, not'
p/ - para 'for, through'
pq - porque 'because'
q - que 'that, which'
qq - qualquer 'any'
rotfl - rebola-se no chão de riso 'rolling on the floor laughing'
tb - também 'also'
tks ou thx - obrigado 'thanks'
x - vez 'time'

_____

_____

_____

_____

DUTCH

& - en 'and'
218 - te laat 'late'
b& - ben 'am'
blk - bleek 'pale'
d - de 'the that'
dk - dat 'that'
dt - dat 'that'
gl - geen 'no'
gep - geen enkel problem 'no problem'
gkcht - gekocht 'bought'
gld - geld 'money'
hb - heb 'have'
ikvou - ik houd van je 'I love you'
ikwniet - ik weet niet 'I don't know'
j - je, jij, jou 'you'
k - ik 'I'
khb - ik heb 'I have'
kmn - komen 'come'
kmt - komt 'comes'
kn - kan 'can'
krgt - krijgt 'gets'
lf - lief 'dear'
m, mn - mijn 'my'
mgge - morgen 'morning'
mkn - maken 'make'
mr, ma - maar 'but'
n, 1 - een 'one'
ngd8 - nagedacht 'thought'

nr - naar 'to, at'
nt - niet 'not'
nwe - nieuwe 'new'
ok - ook 'too'
oppt - oppie toppie 'just perfect'
ovr - over 'about, over'
r - er 'there'
s - is 'is'
tis - het is 'it is'
v, vn - van 'of, from'
vl - veel 'much'
vm - van mij 'from me'
vor, vr - voor 'before, for'
vrdr - verder 'further'
vrlfd - verliefd 'in love'
wrm - warm 'warm'
zvl - zoveel 'so much'

_____
_____
_____
_____
_____
_____
_____
_____
_____
_____
_____
_____

FINNISH

al - akku loppuu 'the battery is running out'
aun - ala unta naa 'dream on'
eos - en osaasanoa 'can't tell you'
et - ei todellakaan 'impossible'
evvk - ei vois vahempaa kiinnostaa 'don't give a damn'
hih - hihitan iteseni henglilta 'laughing to hell'
jk - henkilokohtainen 'personal'
hy - hyvaa yota 'good night'
jks - jarjen kaytto sallittua 'common sense permitted'
miso - missa olet? 'where are you'
misume - miten sulla menee 'how are you'
mrs - mina rakastan sinua 'I love you'
tmy - tule meille yoksi 'will you come back for the night'
tt - terkkua tutuille 'greetings to all'

_____

_____

_____

_____

_____

_____

_____

_____

_____

_____

SWEDISH

3vlig - trevlig 'nice'
7k - sjuk 'sick'
asg - asgarv 'big laugh'
bsdv - bara sa du vet 'just so you know'
cs - ses 'see you'
d - du/dig/din/det 'you, it'
d1a - detta 'this'
dt - det ' it'
e,r - ar 'is'
eg - egentligen 'really'
f1 - fett 'cool'
fr - fran 'from'
hare - ha det bra 'take care'
iaf - I alla fall 'in any case'
iofs - I och for sig 'actually'
ivg - I varje fall 'anyhow'
lixom - liksom 'like'
lr, elle - eller 'or'
mkt - mycket 'much'
ngn, non - nagon 'someone'
ngt - nagonting 'something'
o, oxa, axa - ocksa 'also'
pok, p&k - puss och kram 'kiss and hug'
ql - kul 'fun'
r - ar 'are'
t - tid 'time'
tfn - telefon 'phone'

tkr - tycker 'think'
x - puss 'kiss'

WELSH

?wt - ble wyt ti 'where are you'
@b - ateb 'answer'
@ch - atoch 'to you'
@f - ataf 'to me'
@t - atat 'to you'
0 - dim 'not'
01ia2 - dymuniadau 'wishes'
01ia2 A1 - dymuniadau gorau 'best wishes'
0N10 - dim yn deg 'not fair'
1ig - unig 'only'
1ryw1 - unrhyw un 'anyone'
8nosa - wythnosau 'weeks'
9 - nain 'gran'
9r - nawr 'now'
bath - rhywbeth 'something'
bo - bod 'be'
bxo - becsio 'worry'
cal - cael 'have'
cdb - cau dy ben 'shut up'
cmru m bth - Cymru am Byth 'Wales forever'
d - wedi 'after'
d1 - wedyn 'afterwards'
fo - hefo 'with'
g3 - garter 'home'
gneud, gnd - gwneud 'do'
gt, oo - gweld ti 'see you'
gtd1, gtw - gweld ti wedyn 'see you later'
gwbo - gwybod 'know'

hlo - helo 'hello'
iwn - iawn 'well'
lla - efallai 'perhaps'
m - am 'for'
m8a - mwytha 'cuddles'
m8o - mwytho 'cuddle'
ma - mae 'is'
mav, MaV - dyma fi 'here I am'
mel - meddwl 'think'
mnd - mynd 'go'
mn nw - maen nhw 'they are'
n - yn 'in'
N2 (3, 4, 5, etc.) - ein dau 'one, two, etc.'
n2 (3, 4, 5, etc.) - ni'n dau 'us two, etc.'
nw - enw 'name'
odd - oedd 'was'
pa - paid a 'don't'
pbl - pobol 'people'
pll - pell 'far'
Q - cyw 'chick'
r - ar 'on'
rbennig - arbennig 'special'
ryw1 - rhywun 'someone'
sio - eisiau 'want'
smai, sumai - sut mae? 'how are you'
st, su - sut 'how'
su - sydd 'is'
sxi - secsi 'sexy'
t - ti 'you'
tav, TaV - ti a fi 'you and me'
tcso - tecstio 'text'

tiv, TiV - ti I fi 'you to me'
v - fi 'me'
w - wyt 'you are'
xxx - swsus 'kisses'

_____
_____
_____
_____
_____
_____
_____
_____
_____
_____
_____
_____
_____
_____
_____
_____
_____
_____
_____
_____
_____
_____
_____
_____

CZECH

bo - nebot 'because'
cj - co je 'what'
csdd - co se da delat 'well, it can't be helped'
ctmb - co to ma byt 'what's that supposed to mean'
dh - drz hubu 'shut up'
dn - dobrou noc 'good night'
dyz - kdyz 'when, if'
hh - ha ha 'ha ha'
hosipa - hovno si pamatuju 'I can't remember anything'
jj - jo jo 'oh yes'
jn - jo no 'ok then'
jsm - jak se mas 'how are you'
jszbz - ja se z tebe zblaznim 'you're going to drive me mad'
kkt - kokot 'prick'
kua - kurva 'whore (as a swear word)'
mkc - musim koncit, cau 'have to go, bye'
mmt, mmnt - moment 'wait a moment'
msf - mej se fajn 'enjoy'
mt - miluji te 'I love you'
mtm - moc te miluju 'I love you very much'
mtr - mam te rad 'I love you'
nj - no jo 'ok then'
nn, ee - ne ne 'no, no'
nvm - nevim 'I don't know'
nz - neni zac 'you're welcome'
o5 - opet 'again'

o5z5 - opet zpet 'back again'
omnm - odepis mi na mobile 'write me back on my mobile'
phd - pohoda 'everything ok'
ptze, pze, ptz - protoze 'because'
sem - jsem 'I am'
si - jsi 'you are'
srsm - seres me 'you're a pain'
szm - jsem zamilovany 'I'm in love'
tj - to jo 'that's right'
tvl, twe - ty vole 'mate, dude'
vpho - v pohode 'that's ok'
z5 - zpet 'back'
zaves - zadny velky srani 'no big deal'
zz - zatim zdar 'bye for now'

_____
_____
_____
_____
_____
_____
_____
_____
_____
_____
_____
_____
_____

CHINESE

+u - jia you 'come on'
555 - wuwuwu 'whimper'
88 - baibai 'bye bye'
b4 - bishi 'despise' or 'before'
bb - baobei 'darling' or 'baby'
bc - baichi 'idiot'
bs - bishi 'despise'
cm - choumei 'show off'
dd - didi 'brother'
ddd - dingdingding 'agree'
dx - daxia 'expert'
gg - gege 'brother'
jj - jiejie 'sister'
kl - konglong 'dinosaur (ugly woman)'
mm - meimei 'sister'
mpj - mapijing 'flatterer'
plmm - piaoliang meimei 'pretty girl'

_____
_____
_____
_____
_____
_____
_____
_____

More Info

NetLingo: The List
available at
NetLingo: The Internet Dictionary

http://www.netlingo.com

- Subscribe to Free Acronym & Jargon of the Day Emails

- Read the Top 50 Acronyms Parents Need to Know

- See the Top 50 Funniest, Most Popular, Business terms

- Get our Blog feed on your Yahoo, Google & Facebook

- Bookmark the Largest List of Text & Chat Acronyms

- View the entire Dictionary and Browse by Category

- Buy this book for your friends, family and colleagues!

- Shop for fun Geek Gifts

- Add Your Own Lingo, and more!

In a world of information overload, where new terms and technology change everyday, NetLingo.com gives you what you need to master your digital domain!

Get a Free Acronym Every Day!

Powered by NetLingo.com, with the largest list of texting,
chat, SMS, and IM acronyms and abbreviations, you can get
a free email with a new acronym in your inbox every day.

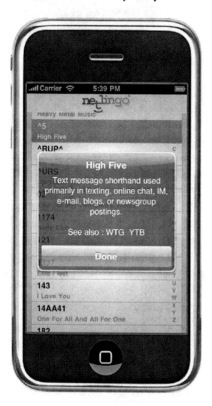

Free Jargon of the Day too!

You can sign up for the free Jargon of the Day too ;-)
How? Easy! Subscribe on the NetLingo website here:
http://www.netlingo.com/subscribe.php

NetLingo is brought to you by Erin Jansen

Founded in 1995, Erin has worked in London, Paris, Munich, New York, Seattle, San Francisco, Silicon Valley, and Los Angeles as a writer, publisher and content specialist. She holds a Masters degree from the London School of Economics and is a graduate of Pepperdine University.

Recognized as a "Top 25 Women in Tech to Watch" and "Top 30 Female Internet Entrepreneur" NetLingo has been featured by more than 100 media outlets including *The New York Times, Wall Street Journal, Fortune, Business Week,* CNN, MSNBC, BBC, Fox News, ABC, NBC, CBS, and the Martha Stewart Show.

See the newest Internet terms at http://www.netlingo.com

To license NetLingo as an educational or marketing tool, or inquire about advertising or press, send email to: info@netlingo.com

CPSIA information can be obtained at www.ICGtesting.com
Printed in the USA
LVOW06s1814130314

377299LV00030B/1119/P